· CONTENTS ·

TWO RECIPES: THE REAL THING

· INTRODUCTION ·

ARE YOU A
DESPERATE GOURMET?

This is not a cookbook for the independently wealthy, the unemployed, or the junk-food junkie. For the rest of us out there who are trying to juggle too many full-time jobs—one paid, the others underappreciated—this book should provide solace at least and culinary resuscitation at best.

The Desperate Gourmet is anyone who loves good food but doesn't have enough time to cook it, and who would like to entertain at home more often if it could be made almost as easy as eating out. The Desperate Gourmet also lives in the souls of those who are not health-food nuts but would still rather not stuff unnecessary chemicals and additives into otherwise healthy bodies. Most of all, the Desperate Gourmet is determined to find original shortcuts for creating gourmet food in almost the same time as it takes to cook up a couple of hot dogs.

After twenty years of stubborn determination, plus two careers of my own (food writing and real estate brokering), my husband's ongoing conducting career, our two children, eleven houses in six cities representing every region of the country, multitudes of our own and other people's dinner parties, I should hope I have learned a few secrets to pass on.

If you buy into the premise that despite all our labor-saving devices, today's cook is a cook in crisis, *The Desperate Gourmet* is for you.

·ONE·

READY OR NOT, HERE THEY COME

"WHO INVITED ALL THESE TACKY PEOPLE?"

YOU'VE just invited eight for dinner. The invitation is long overdue. What's that? You say you feel an out-of-town emergency coming on?

It's not that you don't like these people. They are actually some of your best friends. You're just feeling overwhelmed at the thought of getting your act together and gearing up for a bona fide dinner party.

First there's the clutter you've been meaning to clean up for weeks. The good china is probably dusty; you have no idea what the bar is out of (probably everything that isn't passé); there are flowers and candles to contend with; and then there are the table linens. Ah yes, table linens. Probably unironed because the last time the cleaner did them you were convinced you were paying his rent for a month. And all that *before* you've tackled the menu, the shopping, or the cooking. Now you can really relate to the genius who printed "Who Invited All These Tacky People?" across all those potholders and apron fronts.

This is definitely desperation time. But fear not. And whatever you do, don't feel guilty. Most of us are overextended and trying to keep afloat with only half a motor, sail, or oar.

So cheer up. Your friends are already impressed that you've taken the initiative to invite them at all, and relieved that you're the one who's stuck with the work. By my standards, you get two stars just for making the phone calls.

The house is a mess? Don't worry. If you don't have a regular maid, you can either call a cleaning service or buy extra candles on the theory that surface clean and candlelight make a terrific team.

The Desperate Gourmet will tell you how to stock your bar so you never have to think about it again, how to be more efficient with the flowers and napkins routine, and how to avoid having to buy fresh flowers for every occasion. You will also learn how to simplify the planning, shopping, and cooking so much that you'll wonder what you were worried about in the first place.

For now, just remember three maxims for successful cooking and entertaining in today's world:

1. **Pamper yourself. You're the only cook you've got.**
2. **Pamper your guests. They're as hassled as you are.**
3. **When all else fails—fake it. Which means: In our service-oriented economy, you can always trade more money for less time.**

PAMPER YOURSELF —YOU'RE THE ONLY COOK YOU'VE GOT

· ·

MOST of the over-thirty crowd I know grew up in families with either a nonworking mother, a full-time housekeeper, or, fossil of fossils, both. By today's standards, all of the above make impossible role models. These days the majority of adult women work outside the home. There are more single-parent households than ever before and more singles keeping house because they are marrying later. No matter which category we fall into, most of us feel lucky to have the same once-a-week maid two weeks in a row.

Considering that most of my friends are both intelligent and decently educated, you would think they would have figured out by now that trying to reproduce their parents' style of cooking and entertaining is about as easy as bringing back parlor games to replace the VCR.

The trouble is, old habits die hard, and role models are even harder to erase, especially without guilt. So many family traditions are unspoken (the good as well as the bad) that sometimes it can take us years to realize we're in a trap.

Take a sit-down dinner for eight, for example. In past generations, many families had maids and cooks, leaving the host and hostess free to assume their proper roles: greeting guests, making introductions, keeping the conversation flowing smoothly, and making sure everyone was served enough food and drink to keep them happy. Those women who didn't have maids but didn't work outside the home could at least shift their household chores around and be at home on the day of the party.

As anyone trying to run a career and a household simultaneously can tell you, two full-time jobs leave you feeling incapable of entertaining yourself, not to mention anyone else. Who in his or her right mind would even try to create the illusion of effortless graciousness in the midst of career and domestic chaos? You guessed it. *We* would. As I said before, role models die hard.

Think back to the last dinner party you gave. Did you work so hard you were ready for bed before the first guests arrived? Or did you run up the national debt paying for precooked food and hired help? Did you spend so much time serving and clearing that you can't even remember who was there?

We are all in a time-versus-money trap, and the stakes for getting out seem very high. We still want to entertain and be entertained graciously in our own and other people's homes (surely our preoccupation with home improvement isn't for ourselves alone). Entertaining at restaurants and private clubs is very nice, but not the same.

The only way to survive is to find shortcuts to streamline the process without destroying it or ourselves.

To do this, we have to become aware of the advantages we have and then learn how to use them to save time and trouble.

1. One of the biggest advantages we have over our parents' generation is that we are not really expected to prepare dinner every night of the week. If you want proof, just count the millions who collapse on some fast-food restaurant's doorstep several times a week. Freed from this daily routine, we gain the ability to be more creative on the days that we do cook.

2. Real gourmet food cooked by other people is becoming so readily available, we can offer our family and friends excellent fare without spending all of our time or all of our money. Various combinations of you and gourmet-shop chefs can be both innovative and time-saving.

3. Service of all kinds is available everywhere. Without much trouble you can find just about anybody to perform almost any task you are too overburdened to perform yourself.

4. Social conventions are so much more relaxed these days, we can feel secure with a casual style of entertaining that would have been un-acceptable in our parents' day.

5. The revolution in kitchen equipment, espe-cially the food processor and the microwave oven, has made it possible for us to create culinary masterpieces in the same time it took our mothers to make mashed potatoes.

6. Gourmet cookbooks are so readily available and so easy to understand that today anyone who can read and follow directions can be a first-rate cook.

7. Many of us have more extra dollars to spend than our parents ever had.

8. If chosen carefully and used judiciously, con-venience foods can help short-circuit lengthy preparation techniques.

9. Our greatly enlarged refrigerators and freez-ers offer us far greater possibilities for pre-paring food in advance.

10. Our penchant for lighter, fresher foods and fewer courses means far less preparation time.

Once we learn how to make all this work to our advantage, we will be able to achieve the only real purpose of gourmet cooking and entertaining: to relax and enjoy our family and friends as much as they are enjoying the fruits of our labor.

PAMPER YOUR GUESTS—THEY'RE AS HASSLED AS YOU ARE

· · · · · · · · · · · · · · · · ·

ONE of the most gracious host-esses I know is a lifelong friend of my husband's family and the widow of the founder and first music director of the Honolulu Symphony. Now in her eighties, Marvell Hart still entertains often, and her parties receive nothing but rave reviews from the wide assortment of interesting people she carefully combines for each party. People like her are the ones to study, for they have obviously perfected the art of successful entertaining, the distilled essence of which is providing others an opportunity to relax and enjoy good food, drink, and conviviality in your surroundings.

Having had many happy occasions to study Mrs. Hart's methods, I have concluded that the secret of her success, and by extension successful entertaining for the overextended, is the following:

Keep it simple, make it special, and serve it so often you don't have to think about it.

What she has done so successfully is to create about half a dozen menus for entertaining that she uses over and over. The interesting thing is that it took me several years to figure this out. So much for the theory that guests will remember what was served to them the last time and look down upon any repetition. The truth is, when the food is good, the service unobtrusive, and the conversation lively, all that will remain in the minds of all but the most unusual guest is a happy glow from a delightful evening.

Serving the same menu enough times that you don't have to worry about it solves many problems, among them:

1. The cooking techniques have been perfected, so you don't have to worry about making mistakes.

2. You have already gotten good reviews on the menu from previous guests, so your sense of culinary security should be in good shape well before your guests arrive.

3. Having served the menu before, you know exactly what special dishes and serving pieces you need to present it attractively and can get them all ready ahead of time.

4. You also know what serving methods work best, so if you have kitchen help, you will be able to explain the techniques in advance.

5. Most importantly, having your act together frees you to concentrate on the most important thing of all: your guests.

This may sound simplistic, but think back on the number of parties you have been to where the host or hostess was so busy preparing for guests in the abstract, the real ones got lost in the shuffle. How often have you arrived at a cocktail party where you didn't know many people and the host or hostess was nowhere to be found?

How often have you been ready to enjoy an evening and, receiving no welcome at the front door, suddenly weren't so happy you came?

Trust me, the initial greeting guests receive can set the tone for an entire evening. It is absolutely essential that the host or hostess be at the door to make guests feel wanted, glad they rushed home to make themselves presentable instead of changing into jeans and staying home, and happy to make an effort to be good company even though it's been a rotten day.

I'm sure you have experienced the same feeling of rejection I have when, despite your busy schedule, you have taken the trouble to find some special gift for the hostess, only to find her absent when you enter the house. Since most hostess presents don't come with cards *because* we expect to be able to hand them directly to the recipient, it's disappointing to have to drop your package unceremoniously on the nearest flat surface, knowing the hostess may never know you cared enough to choose something you thought she'd enjoy.

If you care enough about people to invite them to your home in the first place, make them feel cared about from the very first moment they make an appearance. And if they are thoughtful enough to bring a little gift, go out of your way to appreciate whatever it is.

One of the best Desperate Gourmet survival tactics for entertaining is to figure out in advance exactly which tasks are possible and which will push you right over the edge. Then use money, unsolicited offers, or accrued favors to accomplish the rest.

·4·

CULINARY PLAGIARY ON A SILVER PLATTER

IN the years before I became a Desperate Gourmet, I was actually a real gourmet, writing celebrity cooking columns for newspapers and magazines and getting paid for leisurely testing recipes in my own kitchen before committing them to print.

Enter one conductor and two little boys (one at a time, thank goodness), and crisis entertaining was suddenly the order of the day. With neither teacher nor instruction manual, I was forced to make up the course in Creative Culinary Crisis Solving—a real challenge when crisis living was taking up more mental and physical energy than I had in the first place.

I will never forget the birth of the Desperate Gourmet. It was the afternoon my husband called from the Honolulu Symphony office to tell me that the violin soloist for his upcoming concert had just arrived and had invited us to dinner.

Instant midweek babysitter being out of the question on such short notice, I knew we couldn't accept his invitation. The logical response would have been to offer regrets for myself and tell Andrew I'd see him after dinner. But I seem to thrive on challenges. Besides, getting to know the great artists of the music world is for me one of the real rewards of putting up with its power politics.

Could I invite the guest artist to have dinner with us? Quickly I surveyed the situation. It was already three-thirty, a definite minus. I happened to have some pork marinating in a lovely Chinese sauce. Very lucky—a definite plus. Our house had a view of Diamond Head clear out to Pearl Harbor—another plus—but it was in no condition to receive someone who had been wined and dined by practically everybody. A large minus.

I had always meant to have a cache of frozen goodies for emergencies like these, but somehow, well. . . . I said yes anyway. I figured if I started that very minute, I might just be able to run the errands, stash the clutter, do the cooking, feed the kids without their feeling rushed to the slaughter, and still come out a reasonable facsimile of a human being—gracious hostess would be pressing my luck—in time for our guest's arrival. I did have the presence of mind to suggest that host and guest have a before-dinner drink downtown.

How did it all work out? Mixed reviews. My husband, who is both biased and tactful, says the evening was a great success. If you ask me, the food and the table were thrown together and it took me more than an hour into the evening to stop thinking I was falling over a precipice.

Of that semidisaster was the Desperate Gourmet born, making me vow that never again would I be unprepared for whatever unexpected guests might cross our threshold in the future.

Had the Desperate Gourmet been around, how different would the scenario have been? Let's remake the movie and see.

- There would have been a D. G. hors d'oeuvre and dessert, neither of which had taken more than a few minutes to make, in the freezer.
- I would either have had the ingredients for a D. G. main course in the pantry, thereby avoiding a trip to the grocery store, or I would have known exactly which local restaurant to call and what to order.

- The bar would have been well stocked to avoid an emergency trip to the liquor store.
- I would have been able to set the table without thinking because coordinated table linens and napkins—clean ones!—would have been ready and waiting.

"The readiness is all" is as appropriate to the Desperate Gourmet as to Hamlet. And culinary plagiary is the best means of transforming culinary tragedy to triumph, especially when you want to create an atmosphere of elegance with less than adequate time and help.

There are three secrets to successful culinary plagiary, the first of which is deciding which corners to cut.

1. Start with the ideal—the at-home dinner in which every item is lovingly prepared, beautifully presented, and graciously served—then work backward until you reach the possible.

Assess the strengths and weaknesses of the situation—what's on hand and where the holes are, who and what will get sacrificed to the time you devote to this culinary project—and on that basis decide which corners to cut. Decide what you can make yourself and how much plagiary you have to commit. Then *do what you can, skip the guilt, and order what you need.*

2. The second secret is knowing the best sources for cutting corners.

If you have only a limited amount of time, spend it on a menu item money can't buy. Don't waste an hour making your own pâté when a little research will turn up a store-bought variety that's every bit as good as yours. Spend half an hour making a fabulous main dish instead. If there's a Chinese restaurant in your neighborhood that makes fantastic fried dumplings, order them for your hot hors d'oeuvre and spend your time on a homemade dessert or a centerpiece.

Make a point of tracking down the best bakery and stock up your freezer once a month. Great breads and rolls will bail you out when you don't have time to make rice or pasta. Mediocre ones won't.

Good ethnic restaurants are wonderful sources for culinary

plagiary. But if you find a great item, keep the source to yourself. Otherwise your treasure will only elicit an "oh, that" response, putting its excitement level on a par with orange Jell-O.

3. The third secret is to acquire the prettiest and most versatile collection of platters and serving pieces you can find to show off your culinary plagiary to perfection.
For example:

- A nicely decorated ceramic quiche pan about the size of a frozen pie shell is perfect for concealing the fact that your homemade quiche has a commercial exterior.
- Painted soufflé dishes in different sizes can be used to camouflage salads made in kitchens other than yours.
- An assortment of platters, with and without raised sides and handles, is essential for presenting the widest variety of plagiarized fare.
- Glass bowls, both modern and antique, are ideal for showing off their colorful contents.
- Hand-decorated stove-to-table ware made of iron and baked-on enamel is lovely for reheating and serving foods cooked on or off your premises.
- Colorful and unusual baskets (these are as much fun to collect as they are to fill and set out) have almost unlimited uses.
- Sauceboats and dishes in various shapes and materials are perfect for showing off Desperate Gourmet sauces.
- Keep an eye out for good-looking serving utensils, none of which have to match your silverware. They help add to the appearance of graciousness.

TAKE STOCK OF YOUR STOCK: THE BAR, CHINA, LINENS, SILVER

JUST for fun, suppose six unexpected dinner guests suddenly parachuted into your life. Assuming you could get the food and beverage service under control, either from your own refrigerator/freezer or the local take-out, would the rest of your act be together?

- Do you have enough clean on-the-rocks glasses and a dozen clean wineglasses?
- Do you have an ironed tablecloth or six attractive place mats and matching cloth napkins?
- Do you have a plant in a pretty pot or an at-

tractive dried flower arrangement for a center-piece?
- Do you have cloth or good-quality paper cock-tail napkins on hand?
- How about unused candles and a pair of can-dlesticks with no caked wax on the outside?
- Do you stock a basic bar with all the stan-dard repertoire and better-than-average-qual-ity bottles of red and white wine?

If you answered yes to all the above, give yourself five stars and apply for a listing in the Michelin guide.

BAR
......

Assuming you're missing a star or two, let's start with the bar. My definition of social security includes being able to say "Come by for a drink" to anybody, anytime, without making an emergency trip to the liquor store. Getting to this happy state assumes knowing what and how much of it to stock.

To see how your at-home bar stacks up, check your supply of the following:

- Two-and-a-half times the number of wine-glasses you think you'll ever use at one time. Many people have switched to wine as their cocktail of choice, and you don't want to have to wash glasses between cocktails and dinner. The extra half is to avoid having to buy another glass every time one gets broken.
- One-and-one-half times the number of on-the-rocks glasses you think you'll ever use at one time.
- At least a six-month supply of good-quality pa-per cocktail napkins, unless you use cloth.
- An ice bucket and tongs or, better still, two—one that serves two to six, the other eight to twenty-four.
- A small cutting board and knife, preferably dec-

orative and used exclusively for cutting lemons and limes.

- A jigger, even if you never use one. Some guest is always lost without it.
- Six-packs of tonic, club soda, ginger ale, Perrier or spring water, wine cooler, cola, lemon-lime soda, and one fruit juice.
- One bottle each olives and cocktail onions, unless no one has asked for a martini in five years; one bottle of Lemon Zest if you don't always stock fresh lemons.
- Vermouth, sherry, brandy, and several after-dinner drinks like Grand Marnier, Drambuie, Kahlua, or whatever your crowd likes. La Grande Passion is a great new addition to the liqueur market, by the way.
- At least two silver, glass, or attractively decorated ceramic pitchers for water and a specialty mixed drink like Bloody Marys.
- Several dozen disposable plastic glasses for very large parties or very small children.
- At least two attractive serving trays—a small one for serving one or two drinks at an intimate gathering and a large one for serving and clearing at least eight glasses at a time.
- Several clean ashtrays or a "Thank You For Not Smoking" sign.
- At least one fail-safe corkscrew. Please don't keep only some fancy thing you alone can work successfully. It's hell on male egos.

If you have more than eight for cocktails fairly often, you might also want to include the following:

- A cocktail fork or two for fishing out olives and cocktail onions
- The fixings for a specialty something, just to make things festive or different—Mai Tai or Margarita mix, for example, and Bloody Mary mix or a special packet of spices for mulling wine

- An attractive cloth (from white linen to brightly printed, depending on your style) for turning an ordinary small table into a help-yourself bar
- Peel-off labels and a marking pen to label pitchers of specialty drinks for large parties ("Bloody Marys" and "Virgin Marys," for example) so the host doesn't have to stand around and explain

Now that your bar is stocked so well you can say "Come for cocktails" to anyone, anytime, how about the china closet? Do you have enough dishes to serve the largest number of guests you are likely to have at one time?

CHINA

Wedgwood china and Waterford crystal make lovely table settings, but handmade pottery and Mexican glass can be just as attractive if that's the real you. People are a lot less stuffy about what's acceptable these days. One of the most gracious hostesses I know sets her table with *no* matching plates, ranging from antique and valuable to just old and pretty, but all collected lovingly from antique stores and yard sales.

My advice to those still in the acquisition stage is to experiment with styles and, when you find one you're comfortable with, play it to the hilt! If you like the country look, don't hesitate to use rough-textured napkins and oversize crockery bowls for serving. Handwoven mats look wonderful under hand-painted or handmade pottery plates. The only look I am allergic to is "Model Home Modern," which says, "Anyone could live here but nobody does."

Auctions, flea markets, house and yard sales, craft shows, church bazaars—all are wonderful places to pick up an interesting serving piece or two when you have time to browse and if, like me, you find these events recreational. My family has a long vacation tradition of tracking down whatever native crafts a region has to offer, and consequently I have a wonderful collection of plates and platters I consider utilitarian works of art.

Spend a few minutes contemplating your dishes. Are they stored where they are easy to get at when you need them? Or could they be rearranged in a more efficient way? Do you have enough plates and platters, serving bowls, trays? Why not start a Christmas list of missing items? Perhaps it could include a few eye-catching pieces to serve some of the "instant" hors d'oeuvres listed in Chapter 16.

Speaking of hors d'oeuvre plates, I have found it very convenient to keep mine in an upper kitchen cabinet near my food preparation area. I have two stacks ranging from silver to wood to china to pottery. After years of having to go into the dining room to get a plate to serve something that was always prepared in the kitchen, I finally decided to get Mohammed and the mountain together.

Another thing I keep close to the refrigerator is a set of eight individual-size soufflé dishes. If you can find some nice ones, you'll invent a hundred uses for them, especially when it comes to Desperate Gourmet hors d'oeuvres that can be made in a batch and frozen for serving at different times. Large soufflé dishes, particularly the hand-painted variety, double perfectly as serving dishes.

**Test drive your own kitchen before your next party.
There must be something you can reorganize so you
can pamper yourself in the future.**

TABLE LINENS

Coordinate your table linens the way you would a wardrobe for a trip. You don't want a collection of single outfits. You want a small collection of mix-and-match items from which you can create many outfits.

For each set of dishes, try to have several tablecloths or mats that will go with two or three different sets of napkins. If you don't want the trouble and expense of white linen, use the more practical wash-and-wear kind. These days the only limitation on color and style is your own imagination. If you can find something eye-catching and unusual, even the simple food you serve on it will seem festive. For those occasions when you choose to use paper napkins, stock up on several packages in colors that complement your linens.

CANDLES

For some reason, it took me years to learn to buy candles by the dozen. If you've ever had to spend time you didn't have making a last-minute dash for candles the day of a dinner party, you can understand my mistake. Another advantage to buying candles by the dozen is that once they're around, you'll find yourself using them to make ordinary dinners more atmospheric.

Extra candles in strategic places around the living and dining rooms can add immeasurably to a party atmosphere. Experiment with your lighting and use a clever combination of wax and electricity.

COCKTAIL NAPKINS

One of the unspoken prejudices I grew up with was that the only acceptable cocktail napkins were made of cloth. In my frantic early household, the cocktail napkins never seemed to have enough yeast to rise to the top of the ironing basket. Finally I got smart. I found some lovely wash-and-wear napkins and copied a friend who for years had been ordering monogrammed paper cocktail napkins from a mail order company. These come bordered in bright red, green, or blue and are both personal and festive.

I also keep a stock of funny paper cocktail napkins for impromptu occasions. Some of my favorite sayings: "Committee: a group that keeps minutes and wastes hours"; "Where there's a will there's a relative"; and "Midlife crisis: When the mortgage payment and the tuition bill equal more than you make." If you look around, it's amazing what amusements you can find to delight even the stuffiest guest.

SILVER

To me, silver is worth its weight in trouble and expense, but I'm on the side of the generation that didn't have to go out and buy it. If my friends didn't get it from their grandmothers, their large weddings stockpiled it for them in place-setting installments.

In the sixties, if it wasn't silver and it wasn't Dansk, it was likely to be a bad imitation of a traditional silver design. Today we are lucky to have a large selection of well-designed flatware that is proud not to be fake anything but real stainless steel.

FLOWERS

Fresh flowers at the hand of an artful arranger are a real joy to behold unless they are blocking your view of the person across the table. If you don't grow your own, ordering flowers for a dinner party can be an annoying addition to the list of things you already don't have time to do.

When all else fails, fake it—remember? I have several tropical plants I had the florist arrange in two of my prettiest antique pots. I keep them around the living room until they are called into service as a centerpiece, which they do beautifully with no advance planning or expense.

In conclusion, the moral of this chapter is:

Once you have taken stock of your stock and filled in the gaps, you can put the whole operation on automatic pilot.

· 6 ·

STAGING COCKTAILS FOR SIX OR SIXTY

HAVING stocked the bar, you are now ready to serve cocktails to the world. How you choose to do this depends entirely on whom you're serving. If it's close friends and you don't mind if they follow you right into the kitchen, skip the ice bucket and get the ice right from its source. You can chat with your guests while you putter around with the proceedings.

SMALL PARTIES

If you've invited six for dinner and you *don't* want them in your kitchen, you can easily create a bar on any convenient surface. Over the years in our various houses, I have used small tables, sideboards, desks, and other free-standing pieces of furniture. What we have at the moment is the best of all but hard to duplicate except in old houses: a butler's pantry the size of a small apartment

kitchen, which we have turned into a wet bar. It has lots of coun-
tertop space and storage cabinets for liquor, glasses, trays, and
all the incidentals.

If you set up your impromptu bar in the room where you are
going to consume the drinks, you can mix them and still participate
in introductions and conversation. Just be sure you have assembled
everything you think you'll need—ice, liquor, glasses, mixers, cocktail napkins—so you won't be distracted by the preparations.

Many people prefer the look of decanters to ordinary liquor
bottles, and if you do, you'll probably enjoy collecting silver or
pewter or ceramic labels to hang on them. If you *always* use only
the best brands, you may find it a real test of your social security to
see if you have the guts to pour Jack Daniels into a decanter marked
"Bourbon" or Beefeater into one generically marked "Gin." (I think
I was forty before I could bring myself to do it!) If you're at the other
end of the spectrum, however, you may want to run right out and
snatch green decanters out of trees.

LARGE PARTIES

When the number of guests is more than six, you'll get stuck at the
bar if you try to do all the serving yourself. At this point, you have
to decide what kind of help you want. You can either hire or prevail
upon someone to bartend or you can set out a serve-yourself bar.
The second is perfectly acceptable as long as it is arranged so
that people can help themselves quickly and get out of the way.

Think about the best place to set up a help-yourself bar. You'll
want people to have plenty of room to stand while waiting to pour
their drinks and enough space to serve themselves comfortably.
Don't worry if you have to move or even *remove* a piece of furniture
to do this.

Put a nice cloth on your "bar" so that spills won't spoil your
tabletop. Arrange things in logical serving order—ice bucket, glasses,
liquor, mixers—and place cocktail napkins where they can be
picked up last. If you are not sure what people will drink, set out
the same number of on-the-rocks and wineglasses as you have
guests.

You may want to set up two separate bars, either in the same
room, if it's large, or in two separate rooms, so that people don't
have to wait in line. Another alternative, which works just fine, is to

drape a large rectangular picnic table with an attractive cloth and bisect a room with it. Then people can help themselves from both sides. This only works for a large stand-up cocktail party because you'll probably have to move a lot of chairs out of the way to make room for it.

Set up the bar far enough away from the hors d'oeuvres so everyone won't congregate in one corner. I usually set all the food out on the dining room table and set up the bar in another room. It forces people to go back and forth and mingle with other guests.

One of the best ways to avoid both boredom and bottlenecks at a serve-yourself bar is to mix up one or two "Specialties of the House" (see Chapter 16) ahead of time. If you set out your specialties attractively (a few lovely pitchers are a worthwhile investment) and label them clearly so you don't have to explain the contents to each guest, you'll find people are delighted to try something new. And since pouring from a pitcher is much faster than mixing something to order, there won't be a line at the bar.

HOW MANY BOTTLES?

HARD LIQUOR For cocktail parties up to twenty-five people, allow one fifth (meaning one bottle containing four-fifths of a quart or 750 ml) of each of the following: vodka, gin, Scotch, and bourbon.

WINE Most cocktail party guests request white wine three times more often than red. For fifteen guests, allow three bottles of white wine and one red. For twenty-five guests, increase the numbers to five bottles of white wine and two red.

MIXERS One liter each of tonic, soda water, and mineral water should be enough for fifteen people, but if your crowd leans heavily toward either Scotch and soda or Perrier and lime, get out an extra bottle of soda or mineral water. Five liters of any combination of the above is about right for twenty-five people.

"SPECIALTIES OF THE HOUSE" If the centerpiece of your cocktail party is premixed Margaritas, Bloody Marys, or Mai Tais, many people will choose it. Allow six ounces per person and enjoy the leftovers the next day.

SOFT DRINKS Start with two liters of cola and ginger ale and one of diet soda for fifteen people; three and two for twenty-five.

BEER Some people don't offer it at all at cocktail parties. If you want to make it available, I suggest a six-pack of 12-ounce cans or bottles for fifteen people. Double the number for twenty-five.

JUICE Just to be on the safe side, allow one quart for every fifteen people.

ICE One pound per person is about right.

SIT–DOWN DINNERS WITH OR WITHOUT HELP

· · · · · · · · · · · · · ·

NO one would argue that the ideal of gracious dining is to be comfortably seated in an attractive setting with proper lighting and fine table appointments and to be offered delicious food at the perfect temperature by people so skilled at serving that their presence goes almost unnoticed. If you have a lovely home and full-time help or if you have engaged a great catering service or have access to a highly skilled waiter, there is no reason you can't approximate the ideal. For those of us missing some combination of time or money to achieve the above, this chapter will provide the secrets and shortcuts to create a respectable facsimile.

Since the guests are your first priority, decide how many you can accommodate with both grace and ease.

Part of this depends on your personality. If playing host or hostess is a role you enjoy and are comfortable with, you can probably make a larger number of people feel welcome in your house at one time.

If you want all your guests to sit at one table, figure out the maximum number your table can accommodate comfortably and refuse to be influenced by how many invitations you owe! Then give some thought to the number of people you are most comfortable conversing with. Some people prefer six; others feel that eight is better insurance against lulls in the conversation, particularly if the host and/or hostess are doing the serving.

In our experience, ten people at a single table is too many for a single conversation and too many to serve without help.

Decide on the ideal method of service for your space and personal style and get so comfortable with it you won't have to think about it while serving.

Space is the real key here. If your dining space is cramped, you may find the best method is to arrange the food on the plates in the kitchen restaurant-style and present each guest with a filled plate. This saves time as well as space and prevents the food from getting cold as each dish is passed around the table to eight people.

A fine alternative to restaurant-style service is what I call the sit-down buffet. Rather than trying to take or pass separate dishes around the table, I set out both the food and the stacked dinner plates on a sideboard or some other piece of furniture in the dining room (or living room if your dining room is cramped), with appropriate serving utensils next to each dish. After the diners have put food on their own plates, they carry them to their places at the dining table, where everything has been set except the dinner plates.

The sit-down buffet is probably the smoothest of the no-help services, provided you watch out for two possible traps:

1. Be sure you find a solution for keeping the food hot. Electric hot trays detract somewhat from the aesthetics of a buffet table, but don't do nearly as much damage as lukewarm food. Even if food is piping hot when you put it out, if you have no way of keeping it warm, it will be cool by the time you offer seconds. Several small

hot pads may be less noticeable than a large hot tray, particularly the new cordless variety. If you entertain often, you may want to invest in a multi-compartment steamer that uses alcohol or Sterno to keep food hot.

2. As soon as you set out hot food and announce dinner, coax everyone over to the buffet table. If you're unsuccessful, only the first will enjoy a hot meal.

Once guests have filled their plates, proceed as you would for a regular sit-down dinner. Since the table will already be set with the napkins, silver and glasses, all you have to do is assign seats. When it's time to offer seconds, you can let those who want them help themselves or you can take or pass around the platters.

Speaking of seat assignments, be sure to decide beforehand where you would like your guests to sit. Some people think it too formal to assign seats, but it's too chaotic not to. Food gets cold while guests flounder around trying to be polite. If place cards aren't your style, memorize your seating arrangement and point people to the seats you've chosen for them. It not only smooths an awkward pause, it tells your guests you cared enough to put them next to someone whose company you thought they might enjoy.

If you don't have help but prefer sit-down dinner service, the only way to protect the conversation is to know in advance who will help serve and clear. If you are a single host, beware. Your guests will probably feel uncomfortable sitting while you do all the work, and unless you are really insistent, you'll end up with more servers than servees. If a baseball team can have a designated hitter, you can have a designated clearer. If you make a deal before the game starts, the service will be unobtrusive and the conversation will continue to flow smoothly.

A well-organized couple can serve a sit-down dinner for eight provided they have decided in advance who is going to serve what and how it will be done. Since it is cumbersome to try to pass several platters around the table at once, guests can be served faster and better if two people walk around the table and hold the platters for the guests. (Remember, "serve from the left, clear from the right.")

Organize now, relax later.

If I had to choose a one-liner for successful entertaining, that would be it. Organization is what makes it possible to pamper yourself and your guests. How does this translate into a dinner party? Doing the following before the first guest arrives:

- Make a list of everything you are going to serve and tape it to the front of the refrigerator. Don't laugh. Every hostess in the world has a story about the salad or whatever that was found dead in the refrigerator the day after the party.
- Cook whatever you can in advance, keeping warm whatever won't suffer. This is where hot trays come in very handy. If something will need last minute reheating, at least let it warm up to room temperature in advance.
- Arrange everything on plates and platters in advance, especially the hors d'oeuvres. If they must be refrigerated until the last minute, put them on their serving dish and cover it with plastic wrap. You can put the special serving knife or fork on the plate too.
- Assemble every last dish you will use. Get out the coffee cups, stack the dessert plates, put the butter on its serving plate, fill the sugar bowl, pour the cream into the right pitcher, fill the coffee maker with water and measure out the coffee, get out the liqueur tray and glasses if you intend to serve them, et cetera, et cetera, and so forth.
- Make sure the kitchen counters are clear so that dishes can be stacked easily once they are brought in.
- Decide who will bring the dirty cocktail glasses and leftover hors d'oeuvres into the kitchen before dinner, because no one will appreciate their company after dinner.

FEELING OVERWHELMED?

If this looks like a lot of work, it is. Which is precisely the reason the Desperate Gourmet has gone to great lengths to ferret out sophisticated recipes that take an average of fifteen minutes to prepare.

To short-circuit the setup and cleanup operations, you can always hire a neighborhood teenager. It's a pleasant and inexpensive way to pamper yourself when you're entertaining, and you deserve it! Once you've had the same person once or twice, you'll hardly have to do any explaining at all. You may end up with a little less cash, but nothing approaching the cost of professional servers. On the plus side, your net worth as a host will increase considerably.

· 8 ·

BUTCHERS, BAKERS, AND CANDLESTICK MAKERS

EVERY professional knows that the most efficient way to use his or her time is to delegate responsibility to others and then give those well-chosen others enough latitude to get the job done. Letting go of responsibility is hard for some of us, but putting part of your entertaining life in the hands of a few well-chosen experts will make you look like a pro and save you immeasurable time and trouble. In other words:

> **If you spend a little time tracking down the best butcher, baker, gourmet carry-out, liquor store that delivers, florist, helpful teenager, and, for state occasions, caterer and bartender, you might even save your own life.**

Once you know you can trust these people and they catch on to what makes you happy, you can make a phone call from the office and come home to the perfect party centerpiece or preselected wines. If you're not a wine connoisseur and you choose the right liquor store, you may not have to do anything more than recite your menu and give them the number of guests and a budget.

One thing you learn when you move many times is how to "audition" the local butcher, baker, and candlestick maker. The obvious downside is that as soon as you have tracked down the perfect whatever, it's time to change cities again!

In doing your research, start by getting recommendations. Ask people who seem to know the difference between the ordinary and the extraordinary. The same names will probably come up often. Then interview the ones who get the rave reviews.

BUTCHERS Ask if they are willing to custom-cut meat the way you like it and do some of the time-saving extras like slicing, boning, wrapping for the freezer, and even delivering. If the independent butchers are too far away or too pricey, try making friends with one of the butchers in supermarket. You never know what services are available until you ask.

BAKERS Track down the best source of French, German, Italian, or any other bread that has a good crust and great flavor and buy extra loaves for the freezer. Good bread is a great substitute for rice or potatoes when you're desperate.

FLORISTS For those occasions when only fresh flowers will do, check around until you find a florist with a talented arranger on staff. If you're going to spend the money, you don't want an arrangement that looks like all the others in a floral arrangement book. Don't be afraid to ask about prices, either. As in any other service, they vary considerably.

GOURMET SHOPS Dinners cooked entirely by other people can get very pricey, but when you're very busy and still want to entertain, letting someone else cook *part* of the dinner can save you from collapse without killing your food budget for the week. If you hate making desserts, or have time to do the main dish but not the salad, consider buying someone else's once you have tracked down the best someone else.

LIQUOR STORES Always use the name of the friend who gave you the recommendation. The management may not mind palming off on you some of the wines that aren't selling, but they won't want to disappoint your good friend who is *their* good customer. Once you get to know a nice salesperson, you'll probably have a pipeline to some good specials. For those desperate times, it doesn't hurt to know of a liquor store that delivers.

NONPROFESSIONAL HELPERS If you can catch them, teenagers are a wonderful resource. For a reasonable price you can buy yourself some much-needed help setting up, serving, and clearing at your larger parties. Especially at cocktail parties where the numbers are larger than the host or hostess can handle, college students can serve as bartenders without the formality or expense of professionals.

CATERERS Most people use caterers, professional waiters, and bartenders only for state occasions, but it doesn't hurt to know who the best ones are. One tip about working with a caterer: always try to incorporate one or two of your ideas into the menu. When you're spending that kind of money, the last thing you want is for someone to walk into your house, take a quick look around, and say, "Oh, they're using so-and-so tonight."

·9·

SECRETS FOR SUCCESSFUL BUFFETS

· · · · · · · · · · · · · · · · · ·

WHEN the price of silver went
through the roof about ten years ago, it did wonders to kill off the
old prejudice that if the silver wasn't out, company couldn't be
coming. What it didn't take with it, unfortunately, was the notion
that if it wasn't a sit-down dinner, it wasn't real entertaining.

Older folks moaned and groaned about the indignity of having
to balance plates and wineglasses on their laps and having to
stand up and serve themselves seconds. And for years we were so
intimidated we thought we couldn't entertain our parents' friends
or our bosses or anyone who wasn't prepared to take us as we
were—that is, without someone to serve the dinner in any but the
traditional way.

So what did we do? We drove ourselves crazy trying to play
both maid and host and in the process fell flat on our guests. But
with a little advance planning and some basic refinement, all this

---

can be avoided so that even those most accustomed to service won't realize they've lost anything in the translation.

First of all, the "Great Plate and Wineglass Balancing Act" must be avoided at all costs. It's unfair to everyone, *especially* the cook, whose dinner doesn't deserve to be turned into a race because no one can sustain a balancing act for very long. Second, unless you and all your guests love stand-up lunch counters, you must provide a seat for everyone. If you think the plate-and-wineglass routine is hard sitting down, standing up it's as gracious as dining at McD's.

CARDINAL RULE 1   Never invite more guests than you can provide chairs for.

Rent folding chairs if necessary.

CARDINAL RULE 2   Provide a flat surface for everyone to eat on.

If each seat cannot be next to a coffee, end, or tray table, the next best thing is to provide lap trays. That way people can at least put their glasses down while they eat.

REFINEMENT 1   Have someone carry around a tray of filled wineglasses to the seated guests so that they don't have to walk across the room carrying both. This is a good job for a teenager, by the way, either yours or someone else's, who can be hired to do any number of tasks at your party for a lot less than a professional would charge.

REFINEMENT 2   It *is* awkward for people to have to interrupt their conversations to make a trip back to the buffet table for seconds. In fact, over the years I have found that most people are either too comfortable or feel too conspicuous to get up and help themselves, but they will cheerfully accept more food when it is brought to them directly. Even if you don't have hired help, you won't have trouble finding a volunteer to help you make the rounds.

ANOTHER SERVING ALTERNATIVE   If your party is large and you have enough space to set up three or four bridge tables, it lends graciousness to the evening (and adds work, of course) to set the tables nicely with coordinated linens, flowers, and candles and let people form their own groups. When the crowd is large and the various tables seat four to six, you can let people choose their own dinner places and partners. Dessert and coffee can be served either way.

FOOD FOR BUFFETS

Since the logistics for buffet service can be a bit tricky, it's a good "pamper yourself" technique to serve food that requires no last-minute preparation and won't suffer from being kept warm for a while. A good "pamper your guests" trick is to limit the main dish to food that can be eaten with a fork alone. See Chapter 18 for ten fail-safe buffet menus.

DESSERT AND
COFFEE SERVICE

If your guests are happily engrossed in conversation, it seems unfair to make them get up again to serve themselves dessert and coffee from the buffet table. You can solve this by clearing the dirty plates quickly and having someone serve the dessert (put on individual plates ahead of time) to each seated guest.

Someone from each group will probably offer to help, and if you accept, you can have that person take in their group's coffee. The easiest way to do this is by having a separate tray for each group set with the right number of coffee cups and spoons, a silver, china, or ceramic coffee pot, and sugar bowl and creamer. If the crowd is large, make the coffee in one oversize electric coffee maker and fill the coffee pots from it at the last minute.

If your party is large enough so that some guests do not get the chance to get to visit with others for most of the evening, you may want to force the groups to reshuffle by serving the dessert and coffee buffet-style. If so, have someone help you clear off the buffet table and reset it with a stack of dessert plates and coffee cups, a serve-yourself dessert, and the coffee, cream, and sugar. Guests will often regroup happily once they have served themselves. If your guests are divided in two different rooms, two dessert and coffee buffet tables might be better.

· 10 ·

REAL MEN CAN MAKE QUICHE

• • • • • • • • • • • • •

"YOU'VE come a long way, baby," and I don't mean the Virginia Slims woman. I'm talking about men—all those real men who only yesterday were turning up their macho noses at the very thought of quiche and today are not only eating it but are out in the kitchen cooking it.

We seem to be in the midst of a male revolution in the kitchen, ironically, but not coincidentally, just when the females of the species are evacuating the area in droves. My single male friends of all ages tell me that the women in their lives have suddenly added cooking to the "I don't do windows" list and that being offered a home-cooked meal at a woman's apartment is about as frequent an occurrence as asking a father for his daughter's hand in marriage.

Being practical by nature and not in favor of starving, men of all ages are taking up the slack. Meaning, who knows? The largest group of Desperate Gourmets in the studio audience might very well be men! Who are they and why are they listening?

YSM (*Young Single Men*), who cook because they are staying single longer and their peers, health clubs, and doctors, not to mention their bodies, have conspired to send them an NMM message: No More McDonald's (or other fast foods high in fat and sodium), at least not every night of the week.

DMC (*Divorced Men with Children*), whose ex-wives would do everything in their power to have their visitation rights revoked if they thought their ex-husbands were stuffing junk food down their children's throats all weekend. Also because a steady diet of eat-out and take-out turns into expensive burn-out after a while.

MMC (*Married Men with Children*), whose working wives are making them offers they can't refuse to share the responsibilities as well as the privileges of the kitchen.

OSM (*Older Single Men*), including Widowers and Never Marrieds, who are giving cooking the old college try because—is there anyone else out there to do it?

When I first heard that men were being backed into the kitchen by desertion, I thought what a rotten deal. Then I sorted through the single men I know and decided we would have heard a gnashing of teeth and a banging of pot lids if they were not amused. Instead, we have heard the ringing of cash registers in houseware departments, gourmet shops, and bookstores where men are entering into this cooking trend full tilt.

Is it possible? Could it be? Has cooking become the hottest new male sport?

For men, most of whom weren't even aware of what was going on in the kitchen while they were growing up, gourmet cooking is a real challenge. It's hard to produce great dishes when the techniques for the most basic ones evade you.

Fortunately, modern machinery has changed the technology so much, the young or uninitiated are in no worse shape than the experienced cooks who don't want to spend endless hours in the kitchen anymore and don't know how to avoid it. The older women I know tell me they need this cookbook as much as their children who have never cooked.

All I can say is we're lucky to be alive now, when for the first time in history, it is possible to have 90 percent fun and only about 10 percent drudgery in the kitchen to produce sensational gourmet results.

For the man who has never cooked but knows exactly how he

wants his food to taste, being a Desperate Gourmet is an even greater challenge than it is for those who can cook but don't have time.

My suggestion for the uninitiated males of the D. G. species is that they begin bolstering their egos by succeeding with a small number of fail-safe D. G. creations that require no particular cooking technique at all. Many of the recipes in Chapter 15 fall into the "If you can read you can cook" category, so it won't be long before you can turn whatever you find particularly appealing into one of your very own "Specialités de la Maison." The following guidelines should help:

1. If you can sauté ground beef and chop tomatoes, you can create the distinctly different and delicious Taco Salad on page 120. All you need to know before you begin is that to sauté beef successfully, you want to break up all the chunks of beef so the meat browns evenly. If you don't own a skillet large enough for the beef to spread out in a single layer, I suggest adding one to your current collection of pots and pans.

2. If you can cook pasta and mix in a few other ingredients, you can impress the gang with Linguine with Pesto on page 66. If you're a novice, just remember not to overcook the pasta and to rinse it after cooking so it doesn't stick together. Buy yourself a large, free-standing strainer or colander if you don't already own one.

3. If you can buy a frozen pie shell and dice ham and cheese, you can cook the real quiche real men used to boycott. See page 71 for the theme and variations.

4. If you can mix crabmeat with a few items that are already in your refrigerator, you can dazzle your guests with a perfect Imperial Crab from page 93.

5. If you can spare three minutes before work to mix up a marinade, you can make the best

Chicken Teriyaki Sandwiches this side of Hawaii. See page 62.

6. If you can wield a wire whisk, you can make Mini Mansions' Lemon Chess Pie (page 143), one of the deep South's best-kept secrets.

7. If you want to make fabulous salads in seconds, whip up a little Lemon-Dill Dressing (page 75) and keep it in your refrigerator at all times.

8. If you want to produce a fabulous dessert without even cooking, check the D. G. No-Cook Desserts in Chapter 19.

9. If you don't own a single machine more modern than the wooden spoon, flip through Part II and see how many gourmet creations you can make without mixers, blenders, or food processors.

10. If you want to astonish the people who always thought you couldn't cook, you can make Authentic Hawaiian Curry if you can cook a turkey breast on top of the stove! See page 111.

Even if you have never cooked a day in your life, take up your wire whisk, stand in front of the mirror, and say over and over, "I'm a Desperate Gourmet."

GET YOUR KID'S FINGERS OUT OF MY CAVIAR!

· · · · · · · · · · · · · · · · · · · ·

THIS title was inspired by the worst guest I ever entertained. Not the two-year-old, but the mother who brought him to an adult cocktail party without asking and silently watched him wreck my prize hors d'oeuvre. I know I'm not alone. In the heart of every hostess lurks a similar experience which, were it not for the victim's tact and gentility, might easily have ended in murder.

In my humble opinion, children and cocktails don't mix. Not even, in the case of the foregoing outrage, if both parents work and feel guilty about not having seen their offspring all day. So would I. But if you really want to spend after-five time with your toddler, skip the party and take him or her to the park. No one ever died from missing a cocktail party—quite the reverse.

What if the party is in *your* home, which also happens to be your children's principal residence? Remember the "pamper yourself'' theory. Hire one of your regular babysitters to take the kids on an outing or play with them anywhere in the house that your guests aren't. The babysitter can parade them around to say a brief hello to the guests and whisk them away before they decide they must have their mother's undivided attention right this minute!

This technique also applies to the "pamper your guests" theory. Chances are, if your guests are paying someone to take care of *their* children so they can relax and enjoy a little grown-up time, they won't appreciate having *your* children to contend with.

If you have small children, you have probably had the horrible experience of getting so absorbed in your fancy dinner preparations, you forgot to feed them. A babysitter will do wonders to solve this problem, too, especially by arriving about five o'clock.

This is when the microwave oven really comes in handy, by the way. I always keep frozen macaroni and cheese or some other lesser of the frozen evils in my freezer. Even our teenagers use them when my gourmet obsession for the party doesn't appeal to them or it isn't ready when they're starving, which tends to be most of the time.

As a mother who always worked *and* entertained fairly often, I am very familiar with the guilt that comes from knowing you are sacrificing your kids to your guests on certain occasions, which is different from the guilt you feel when you're working. Most mothers work these days, and entertaining is often optional. But if you really follow the advice in this book, I think you'll reduce the entertaining guilt to a tolerable level. Especially if you enjoy the preparation and find ways to let your children share in the fun.

· 12 ·

THE DESPERATE GOURMET PLAYS WEEKEND HOST

WELCOME to "Who Invited All These Tacky People?" again, only this time you've really done it. Gotten yourself into not one but multiple meals, sheets, towels, and maybe even that worst of overnight evils, the shared bath. Okay, genius, how are you going to carry off the gracious weekend host routine when you have barely enough energy to get home on your own steam by the time five o'clock Friday rolls around?

First of all, you're not going to pretend you have nothing to do except play the perfect host. Second, you're going to stock the refrigerator with a weekend's worth of Desperate Gourmet supplies so you spend no time in the grocery store and not much more in the kitchen while your guests are around. Third, you're going to establish some simple ground rules so the stress factor for both parties never gets above par.

If you have been an overnight guest more than once or twice, you have probably had the awful experience of staying with people who didn't give you a clue about the inner workings of their world. Is it every man for himself in the morning, or will the host be hurt if you don't show up at a certain time for breakfast? Will the host be relieved or hurt if you have a weekend agenda of your own? Should you ask for an extra blanket if you're cold or freeze in silence for fear the host will think you're calling him a cheapskate for not keeping the house properly heated? If it's your accustomed cocktail hour and cocktails are not forthcoming, should you ask for a drink or simply help yourself to the bar?

These little questions loom larger than they should when no life-style instructions come with the hospitality. And you'll never know whether the host hasn't offered them because he doesn't care what you do, does care but hasn't thought enough about it to articulate it, or cares very much and won't tell you he's offended because he doesn't want to appear bossy. Unfortunately, all the above are possible!

Everyone's life-style is different, but here are a few ground rules that have worked for us over the years. Choose whatever is appropriate and make up the rest.

SUGGESTED GROUND RULES
FOR THE WEEKEND HOST

1. Tell your guests what time you have breakfast and invite them to join you *if* the hour suits them. Show them where things are so they can help themselves if they're up earlier or later than you are.

2. Coordinate schedules right from the beginning. Ask your guests if they have any special plans so you'll know when not to expect them. If you'd like to give a cocktail or dinner party in their honor, clear the date and time well before they arrive. If they want to take you out to dinner one evening, they'll probably tell you about it at the same time so you can accommodate their request.

3. Establish transportation ground rules right from the start. If guests are flying in and will be stranded without a car, tell them in advance if you will be able to lend them one of yours and, if not, make sure they know they'll need to rent one. If so, they might want to pick it up at the airport, but you may have to suggest it. If they are driving, ask what time they think they will be arriving and let them know if you are planning a special meal when they arrive. It's like O. Henry's "Gift of the Magi" when you've planned a special meal but haven't told your guests and they've just stopped for dinner so as not to inconvenience you.

4. If something unavoidable or unusual will be going on in your life while guests are visiting, tell them in advance so they can either participate or avoid it.

5. Give guests a house key—the more freedom and flexibility you both have, the lower everyone's stress level—but be honest about telling them if it will disturb you to have them come home later than a certain hour.

6. If a guest is going to have to share a bath, tell him or her what time the bath is likely not to be free in the morning.

7. Ask guests if they have any special food quirks or allergies before you shop for the whole weekend.

8. If your guests are bringing small children, tell them if you have easy access to any special equipment like cribs or playpens.

9. Tell them honestly if you appreciate help in the kitchen or if you work faster without others underfoot. If they seem lost without an assignment, try to find something for them to do.

10. Try to anticipate what guests might need so they don't have to ask for it. Put extra pillows, blankets, and towels in the guest room closet and a supply of items they may have forgotten—toothbrushes, toothpaste, disposable razors, shaving cream, shampoo, deodorant, aspirin, bath powder, even a blow drier—in an accessible place. Your guests will appreciate the thought even if they haven't forgotten a thing. Being a weekend host is an art, and no matter how busy you are or how limited your space, your welcoming attitude and the time you spend with your guests is far more important than whether you can offer them maid service.

11. Guests are always grateful to find a small collection of well-chosen books and magazines in their rooms, particularly if the books include a bestseller they might not have read yet and a current publication that lists goings-on about town. We always include a map and whatever local lore might be of interest to a guest in search of a little midafternoon quiet.

THE DESPERATE GOURMET'S WEEKEND KITCHEN

A little advance planning is all you need for a carefree weekend —at least in the food department. You'll be fine as long as you make a pact with yourself not to do any shopping and as little cooking as possible while houseguests are under your roof.

If the weeknights prior to your guests' arrival are so jam-packed you can't play cook-and-freeze or cook-and-refrigerate, don't worry. This is the time to employ Desperate Gourmet Maxim 3: "You can always trade more money for less time." The last thing you want to do is sacrifice people you like and don't see very often to mundane kitchen tasks. So open your wallet and buy the best gourmet takeout that local shops have to offer. You can always add a few items of your own to placate your conscience. If you do have a little preparation time before the arrival of houseguests, look over the ten-minute Desperate Gourmet dishes in Chapters 15, 16, and 19.

For maximum flexibility and minimal stress, don't try to plan each meal down to the last detail or you may be unpleasantly surprised by who does or doesn't turn up at the table. Try to buy ingredients that are so versatile you don't have to care.

BREAKFAST SUGGESTIONS One of the pleasures of traveling is not having to fix your own breakfast, so even if your guests' morning schedule doesn't coincide with yours, try to set out attractive help-yourself platters of fresh fruits and a choice of breakfast specialties. In addition to cereal, I like to offer the kind of pastries most people don't treat themselves to on ordinary mornings at home.

This is when I use local specialty stores the most, stocking up on the best coffee cakes, muffins, croissants, Danish pastry, homemade jam, and tea biscuits I can find. If I have time to make my own specialties, of course I prefer it. But if not, I happily let someone else's fingers do the baking.

If I know our guests will be joining us for breakfast, I usually fix one of our family specialties just to let them know their visit is a special occasion. Naturally my breakfast specialties are simple enough to be whipped up while everyone is still on their first cup of coffee.

Here are some pointers to keep in mind when planning the weekend meals:

- If your guests are friends you haven't seen for a while, you will probably want to extend the cocktail hour or linger over dessert and coffee. Take this into consideration when making your shopping list. Lay in all the wine and spirits you think you'll need for the weekend and check the ingredients for the hors d'oeuvres and desserts you plan to make. Too busy to make anything? Check the list of pop-top hors d'oeuvres that taste homemade in Chapter 16 and pay a visit to the best bakery in town.
- If your guests will have to forage for a meal while you're out, give them a mini-tour of the refrigerator before you leave. It's a kindness to them and saves you from coming home and finding they have eaten the very thing you were saving for dinner.
- If you are planning a dinner party for your houseguests while they are in town, try to do all or most of the cooking before they arrive. Don't

try to play Superman. The moment the pressure starts making you wish they weren't coming, bite the financial bullet and reschedule your dinner party at a restaurant. Your sanity is more valuable than whatever the cost.

- A few suggestions for food to have on hand when weekend guests are expected: Lentil Soup with Beer or Black Bean Soup Borracho, which keep for at least a week in the refrigerator and are so thick they're a meal; Linguine with Pesto made from a magic little jar that's right in your pantry; Two Spinach/Sausage Quiches that will go from freezer to oven anytime; Chicken Teriyaki Sandwiches made from boneless chicken breast, which cooks in three minutes, and lots of similar recipes you will find throughout Part II.

- And of course, if you follow my lead and keep one Desperate Gourmet hors d'oeuvres and dessert in the freezer at all times—my choices are Homemade Boursin and Intoxicated Mud Pie—you will feel a lot less desperate about inviting guests for the weekend at all.

·TWO·

RECIPES: THE REAL THING

· 13 ·

EQUIPMENT: THE BARE ESSENTIALS

AS you might have guessed, I am not a purist. I consider almost no culinary accoutrement sacred and enjoy but do not worship the microwave oven. The only machine I would not be without is the food processor, mainly because I find it a bore to chop large things into little pieces and to puree anything by hand. I mix all batters in the food processor, grate cheese (there is no comparison between freshly grated Parmesan cheese and the shredded cardboard that comes in cans), chop herbs, slice onions, make sauces and homemade soups in seconds, and so on. I would also be very sad if someone took away my wire whisk or my favorite knives.

As for the microwave, I rarely use it for cooking much more than vegetables (I think it cooks the fresh varieties without water better than any other method), but I find it very good for defrosting, softening or melting butter, reheating soups or stocks, or warming rolls right in their baskets. It is also invaluable for heating up leftovers right on the serving plate. Someday I may learn to cook chicken or bake bread in the almighty machine, but I haven't yet felt the need.

Do I recommend owning one? Absolutely. For all the above reasons and especially if you have kids. Even the impatient ones (are there any other kind?) will spend an extra minute heating up soup for a snack instead of taking to the salt mines of the ubiquitous chip. And while we're on the subject, when you're entertaining, you can feed the kids from the microwave while you're playing gourmet for the grown-ups in the regular oven.

Can you use this cookbook without a microwave? Sure. Without a food processor? This is your life, Desperate Gourmet, but the time you waste will be your own. Is it a lot simpler to use than it looks? Absolutely. If you'll dust it off (those of you who are married and between twenty and thirty probably got one as an engagement or wedding present), I'll show you how to become an instant gourmet.

As for other equipment, I assume you have a set of good, heavy pots and pans and the usual collection of baking tins. If you think you're missing a few or want to replace some, a restaurant supply store is a wonderful place to go to fill in what you don't have. Most will sell to ordinary folk like you and me, and their products are built to last far longer than the supermarket variety.

Any good cook will tell you that the last place to cut corners is on kitchen knives. It's amazing how many people limp along with inferior knives or knives that haven't been sharpened since the neighborhood knife grinder went out of business. Buy the best available and they'll last a lifetime. Keep them sharp and watch your preparation time shrink to "possible" from "out of the question." What are the bare essentials? For starters, try paring, boning, large French chef's, and basic utility knives.

Test drive your own kitchen while you're cooking to see if you have enough mixing bowls, measuring cups (it's amazing how much time an extra one or two can save), baking dishes attractive enough to go to the table, good-quality cooking utensils, and anything else that is either missing or is ready for retirement.

While you're up, test drive the kitchen for efficiency. Take a few minutes to look closely at the cabinets you've chosen to store things in. Does the arrangement of pots, pans, dishes, and pantry give you the maximum convenience for the least number of steps? If planning space isn't your forte, offer to feed a friend dinner in exchange for helping you figure it out. A few minutes of rearranging could save you hours of inconvenient reaching.

People seem to spend more time organizing their closets than their kitchens these days, but most of us still spend more time cooking than dressing.

· 14 ·

THE DESPERATE GOURMET'S BASIC PANTRY

· · · · · · · · · · · · · · · · · · ·

One of the trade secrets of the Desperate Gourmet is a small collection of ingredients that can be found right on the shelves of your supermarket if you try a large, well-stocked chain. If not, you may have to check out a few ethnic grocery stores but trust me, it's worth it.

Being a Desperate Gourmet has led me to collect certain ingredients for dishes that make people marvel while I relax. To keep the list manageable, I have not included either the obvious, like salt and pepper, or the specific, like chick peas, which are used to make only one recipe in this book. If you love hummus and want to be able to make it from ingredients right in your pantry, you can decide never to be without a can of chick peas.

HERBS AND SPICES

basil
bay leaves
caraway seeds
chili powder
cinnamon (ground)
cloves (ground)
coriander
cumin
dill weed

ginger (ground)
marjoram
mint
oregano
red pepper
sage
tarragon
thyme
vanilla

OTHER SEASONINGS

Dijon-style mustard
ketchup
minced garlic (in a jar, packed in oil)
Worcestershire or Pickapeppa sauce
Kikkoman or other good-quality soy sauce
pesto sauce (in a jar)
mirin (sweet rice wine for cooking)
tahini
Tabasco sauce

STAPLES

baking powder
baking soda
brown sugar
butter
chicken bouillon cubes
cornmeal
cornstarch
corn syrup
crackers (two kinds)
dill and/or basil in season (fresh)
eggs
flour

Greek or Italian olives
honey
lemons
long-grain rice
mayonnaise
mushrooms (dried)
olive oil
Oriental sesame oil
Parmesan cheese (chunk or freshly ground)
parsley (fresh)
peanut oil
pie shells (frozen)
red wine vinegar
rice wine vinegar (optional)
tarragon vinegar
tomato sauce with herbs
tortellini (fresh)
vegetable oil
white sugar

SPIRITS

brandy or cognac
dark rum
Kahlua
Marsala wine
sherry
white wine

POP-TOP HORS D'OEUVRES

canned caponata
herring fillets in mustard, beer or tomato sauce
macadamia nuts
natural carrot chips
Romanoff black lumpfish caviar (2-ounce jar)
smoked almonds
smoked oysters, baby clams, or mussels

Strasbourg Pâté Maison (7-ounce can)
stuffed dolma (grape leaves)
Tarama Solata (in a jar)
whole baby corn (15-ounce can)

Here is a list of the less-than-ordinary ingredients for recipes in this book. You may want to get your hands on whatever you don't already have in the house so that you aren't caught off guard just when you're ready to start trying a recipe. Once purchased, you won't have to think about the majority of these items for months.

GINGER ROOT Buy a piece about two inches long, peel and shred it. If you then put it in a covered jar and fill the jar with dry sherry or vodka, you can keep it for months in the refrigerator. If that sounds too much like work, use ground ginger instead.

CHOPPED GARLIC IN OIL This is the Desperate Gourmet's best friend. It is freshly chopped cloves of garlic preserved in oil. It comes in a jar and will keep indefinitely in your refrigerator. Substitute one teaspoonful every time a recipe calls for a freshly chopped clove of garlic and no one will know you didn't peel and chop it yourself. When my recipes say "1 teaspoon minced garlic," this is what I mean.

PARMESAN CHEESE If you don't have a food processor to grate this flavorful hard cheese, please find an Italian grocery that will grate it for you. The grated cardboard that comes in little cans will not do justice to a gourmet recipe, desperate or otherwise.

FRESH TORTELLINI Many supermarkets are now stocking these lovely little filled pastas in one of the refrigerator sections of the store. Finding out where it is hidden may take some doing, but ask before assuming the store doesn't have it.

GREEK OR ITALIAN OLIVES If the deli section of your supermarket doesn't sell these in bulk, you'll have to find an ethnic grocery store that does. The round black things that come in cans marked olives are unworthy of the name.

PICKAPEPPA SAUCE   This wonderful creation is sort of a cross between Worcestershire sauce and chutney. It hails from Jamaica and contains tropical tamarinds and mangoes. My local supermarket stocks it, but if yours doesn't, use Worcestershire instead.

PESTO SAUCE   Great if you can find a good brand like Polli, but if you can't, buy a jar of dried basil and use the recipe in this chapter to make your own almost instant.

VERY-GOOD-QUALITY OLIVE OIL   My favorite is Apollo brand, which is made from Calamata olives and imported from Greece, but ordinary grocery stores don't stock it. When I'm too busy to get it at my local Greek and Italian grocery, I pick up Pompeian at the supermarket, and it's almost as good.

GOOD-QUALITY RED WINE AND TARRAGON VI-NEGARS   There are lots of good brands out there. Buy several different kinds at once and try them out.

TAHINI   Buy this only if you intend to make Falafel. Tahini is made from ground sesame seeds and is something of an acquired taste. I thin it with mayonnaise or mix it with mashed avocado for an unusual sandwich spread with lettuce and tomato. If you don't think you'll use it more than once, don't bother with it.

15

LIGHT SUPPERS/ SUNDAY BRUNCHES: AN EASY WAY OUT

ONE of the more intimidating features of the weekend dinner party is that it is designed to provide an entire evening's entertainment. Stage a mediocre performance and you have done in a large portion of your guests' high-season free time. The good news about an invitation for Sunday brunch, midweek supper, or light supper before or after a movie, lecture, concert, or the theater is that no one expects it to be the important event of the day.

With the pressure of staging a major production off, you can enjoy your guests in a more relaxed setting. The food still has to be top quality, but the greater simplicity of the occasion is manna for the Desperate Gourmet. If you also happen to be a novice cook or your entertaining routines are a little rusty, a light supper from this chapter might be the perfect place to begin.

What's appropriate? Interesting combinations of light food, including main-dish pastas, salads, and soups. Add the Desperate Gourmet's special criteria and you have almost instant creations with great flair and unusual flavor.

What follows is a collection of Desperate Gourmet light specialties that need only the addition of a simple salad and some old-fashioned crusty bread to put sixteen light supper menus right into the mainstream of your repertoire.

A WORD ABOUT CRUSTY BREAD Find a good European or ethnic bakery, even if it's clear across town, and stock up for the freezer because there is no substitute for good bread! Also try the Desperate Gourmet Irish Soda Bread in this chapter. It can be mixed with the fingers in five minutes with no kneading!

A WORD ABOUT SALADS When desperation strikes, I know I can always whip up a great green salad with rabbit food and one of my two favorite D. G. dressings, Lemon-Dill or Tarragon Vinaigrette. I keep one or both in my refrigerator at all times because they can be mixed up in minutes and will keep for several months. Both recipes are in this chapter, so keep reading.

ABOUT THE FOOD PROCESSOR You don't need one to produce these recipes, but slicing and chopping by machine is a great boon to the Desperate Gourmet. In the following recipes, I use my food processor wherever it says chop or slice. If you don't have a food processor, be sure you do have a well-sharpened knife.

Note: All recipes serve six unless otherwise stated.

SPINACH FETTUCINE WITH SAUSAGE AND BOURSIN

This 10-minute creation is fresh and different. Use the Boursin you make in a batch for hors d'oeuvres in Chapter 16 or use store-bought Boursin if you don't have any on hand. Buy good-quality fresh bulk sausage and add a little fresh or dried sage if it seems too bland. Buy the best-quality fettucine noodles you can find. The difference is noticeable.

½   **pound spinach fettucine noodles**
1   **onion**
1   **green pepper**
3   **hard-ripe tomatoes**
1   **pound bulk sausage**
6   **ounces Boursin cheese**

1. Cook and drain the fettucine.
2. While the noodles are cooking, thinly slice the onion, green pepper, and tomatoes.
3. Brown the sausage (in a tiny bit of oil if it doesn't have enough fat) with the vegetables and drain.
4. Mix in the noodles and Boursin and heat through.

CHICKEN TERIYAKI
SANDWICHES

It takes just 5 minutes to create these sandwiches, *including* the home-made teriyaki sauce, which is infinitely better than the bottled variety. If you have time to marinate the chicken in the sauce for a few hours or overnight, that's great. If you're really desperate, you can cheat by dou-bling the amount of the sauce and no one will know the difference!

A word about cornstarch: If you don't want lumpy sauce, mix the cornstarch into 2 or 3 tablespoons of the hot sauce first, then add it to the remainder, heating and stirring the sauce until it is thick.

Sauce:
1   **cup soy sauce**
1   **cup *mirin* or sherry**
1   **tablespoon Oriental sesame oil**
1   **tablespoon shredded fresh ginger or 1 teaspoon ground ginger**
1   **teaspoon minced garlic**
1   **tablespoon cornstarch**

3   **whole skinned and boned chicken breasts (about 1½ pounds), cut in half**
2   **to 3 tablespoons peanut oil**
6   **sesame seed buns**

1. Mix the sauce ingredients (except the cornstarch) together and marinate the chicken 4 to 8 hours, or double the sauce and don't marinate the chicken.
2. Heat a little peanut oil in a heavy skillet and sauté the chicken (drained) about 2 minutes on each side.
3. Heat the sauce until hot in a microwave oven or on top of the stove and thicken with the cornstarch.
4. Toast the buns lightly. Lay each chicken breast on half a bun, spoon the sauce on top, and cover with the other half bun.

SMOKED HAM WITH THREE D. G. SAUCES

A thick slice of good-quality smoked ham is delicious any time of day, particularly if it's been heating in a slow oven for a few hours. Since smoked hams are fully cooked, however, you can serve them at room temperature with a lovely sauce warmed in the microwave or on top of the stove and receive rave reviews for cleverness and virtually no work.

Try to pick a good-quality smoked ham that is pink in color and doesn't have too much excess fat. I've had very good luck with Cook's brand, which I have seen in supermarkets as far apart as New York and Texas. Of course there are some superb smoked hams that can be ordered by mail, but they are not inexpensive.

The combination of ingredients is the secret to these sauces. Serve a platter of ham slices by themselves or garnished with fruit and pass one, two, or three sauces separately.

GUAVA-BRANDY SAUCE

Good-quality brandy (Courvoisier or Napoleon, for example)
Guava jelly
Pinch ground cloves

Make any amount you like by mixing a teaspoon of brandy into each tablespoon of guava jelly. Start with a pinch of cloves and add more to taste. Serve warm.

ORANGE FLOWER SAUCE

Top-quality orange marmalade
Orange flower water (available in liquor stores)
White vermouth

To each 2 tablespoons of marmalade, add 1 teaspoon orange flower water and 1 tablespoon vermouth. Serve warm.

BOURBON-CHUTNEY SAUCE

1 8- or 9-ounce jar chutney
2 teaspoons bourbon

Mix and serve warm.

IRISH SODA BREAD

Since the ham sauces are so simple and the smoked ham needs no cooking, even the most desperate gourmet might find time for this healthful, quick, and delicious Irish Soda Bread, which will complement the ham wonderfully and impress the guests. Aside from its great crust and full-bodied flavor, its best feature is that it requires no kneading and can be mixed with a wooden spoon!

2 cups whole wheat flour
1 teaspoon salt
2 teaspoons baking soda
¼ cup sugar
1 cup buttermilk
1 beaten egg
¼ cup (½ stick) butter, melted
¾ cup raisins

1. Preheat the oven to 450°F.
2. Stir the dry ingredients together.
3. Mix the buttermilk, egg, and butter and add gradually to the flour mixture. Stir in the raisins.
4. Shape the dough into a round, flat loaf and cut a deep X across the top.
5. Bake on a flat pan for 45 minutes.

ZUCCHINI LASAGNA

This lasagna is a delicious change from lasagna with meat and a special treat for your vegetarian friends. Because you can cook it in the microwave without precooking the noodles (a major breakthrough!), it is part of the Desperate Gourmet's almost instant repertoire.

About the cheeses: I have said this before, but I'll say it again. I am against the grated cardboard called Parmesan cheese that comes in little cans. There are enough good cheese stores or Italian groceries all around the country that it shouldn't be too hard to find freshly grated Parmesan or Romano without additives. Or you can buy a chunk of Parmesan cheese in the supermarket and grate it yourself. The Italian grocery store near me also sells homemade mozzarella that is out of this world. See if you can find some.

About tomato sauce: Really desperate gourmets do not make tomato sauce, but they don't like the taste of canned either. Solutions? Buy the packaged *fresh* tomato sauce sold in some stores or pour about a third of a bottle of Blanchard and Blanchard's tomato basil dressing into canned tomato sauce. If you can't find that, add to three 15-ounce cans of tomato sauce: 2 tablespoons red wine vinegar, 2 tablespoons olive oil, 1 tablespoon lemon juice, salt, garlic and onion powder to taste, and half a jar of dried basil. Last *and* least: Use canned tomato sauce with herbs.

3	**15-ounce packages fresh tomato sauce**
½	**pound lasagna noodles**
3	**medium or 4 small zucchini**
½	**pound mozzarella cheese**
15	**ounces ricotta cheese**
½	**cup freshly grated Parmesan cheese**
½	**jar dried basil**

1. Pour the tomato sauce into an oblong microwave-safe dish and push the lasagna noodles down into the sauce. Cook on high for 10 minutes.
2. Meanwhile, thinly slice the zucchini and mozzarella. Remove half the lasagna noodles from the dish and all the sauce except enough to coat the bottom.
3. On top of noodles layer half the zucchini, half the tomato sauce, half the mozzarella, ricotta, and Parmesan cheeses, and half the basil. Place the remaining noodles on top and repeat the layers.
4. Cook 10 minutes on high, covered with plastic wrap. Let stand 5 minutes, covered, before serving.

RUSSIAN BORSCHT ÉMIGRÉ
•••

Simmered slowly for hours, borscht is one of the real delights of a cold winter's day. The Desperate Gourmet version has shortcuts that are so subtle they have fooled some real purists. Preparation time is 5 to 10 minutes; cooking time 1 hour without any watching or stirring. Make it the day before you want to serve it, and it will taste even better.

1	1-pound can sliced beets
1	1-pound jar sliced pickled beets
½	head cabbage, coarsely shredded
4	large potatoes, peeled and sliced
1	cup red or rosé wine
3	bouillon cubes dissolved in 3 cups water
¼	cup red wine vinegar
2	teaspoons caraway seeds
2	tablespoons minced fresh or 2 teaspoons dried dill
1	tablespoon sugar
	Salt and pepper to taste
1	cup sour cream

1. In a large saucepan or flameproof casserole, put all the ingredients except the sour cream.
2. Bring to a boil, then simmer, covered, for 1 hour.
3. Serve hot and pass the sour cream on the side so that guests can mix in about a tablespoon if they choose.

LINGUINE WITH PESTO
•••

If the occasion demands something more substantial than borscht, bread, and salad, you might want to add Linguine with Pesto, especially if you have discovered one of the excellent pesto sauces now on the market in jars. My supermarket stocks an Italian import called Polli, which everyone thinks is homemade. With linguine and a jar of pesto in my pantry and a loaf of good Italian bread in my freezer, I can produce a nice little supper on the spur of the moment.

If you can't find good pesto, don't worry. It's not very hard to make your own. And its uses go way beyond pasta. Try a little on sliced tomatoes or make open sandwiches by spreading a little pesto on Italian bread and top with slices of mozzarella and sun-dried tomatoes.

1	jar dried basil leaves (or 2 cups fresh leaves)
2	teaspoons minced garlic
1	teaspoon salt
3	ounces pine nuts
2	tablespoons freshly grated Parmesan or Romano cheese
¾	cup olive oil
1	pound linguine

1. Mix all the ingredients except the linguine in a food processor or blender or chop by hand and set aside.
2. Cook the linguine in about 6 quarts of boiling water with a little salt, drain, and toss with a little additional olive oil.
3. Toss the linguine with the pesto sauce and serve with additional grated cheese on the side.

LENTIL SOUP WITH BEER

Another interesting way to augment a soup supper is by serving it side by side with another soup of contrasting texture and flavor. An excellent twosome is Russian Borscht Émigré and Lentil Soup with Beer. My Aunt Lillian makes a very flavorful version with kielbasa or smoked sausage that is so thick it's a meal in itself. A cup rather than a bowl will pair up happily with a cup of the lighter, more liquid borscht. Both the colors and the flavors complement one another. While fiddling around with the recipe one day, I discovered that replacing about 12 ounces of the beef stock with beer gave the soup even more flavor without the actual taste of beer.

This Desperate Gourmet loves lentil soup because the lentils can be soaked while you sleep and cooked without stirring and the soup keeps in the refrigerator about a week without losing any flavor.

There are two ways to serve this soup, depending on the thickness you prefer. If you like it more like a stew, with almost no liquid, use less water when you cook it and serve it with croutons and a small pitcher of wine vinegar on the side. If you prefer it more souplike, skip the vinegar and croutons.

1	pound dried lentils
3	stalks celery
3	carrots
1	onion
2	to 3 tablespoons olive oil
2	to 3 tablespoons minced fresh parsley

2	tablespoons minced fresh or 2 teaspoons dried dill
1	pound kielbasa or packaged smoked sausage, sliced
12	ounces (1 can) beer
2	teaspoons beef bouillon
2	cups water

1. Soak the lentils overnight or boil 2 minutes in 8 cups water and let stand for an hour. Drain.
2. Slice the celery, carrots, and onion and sauté them lightly in olive oil in a heavy skillet or in the microwave for 2 minutes on high.
3. Combine the lentils, vegetables, and remaining ingredients in a stockpot or heavy flameproof casserole. Bring to a boil and simmer, covered, for 1 hour.

BLACK BEAN SOUP BORRACHO

If you're looking for a little more drama, black beans have a much deeper color and a wonderful satiny sheen when cooked. You can use the same ingredients as for the lentil soup above, but substitute black beans for the lentils and a little bacon for the kielbasa.

To serve it southwestern style, call it Black Bean Soup Borracho and top it with a dollop of sour cream and a bit of chopped tomato and fresh coriander, which is also known as *cilantro* or Chinese parsley. If you live in a part of the country where Mexican food is popular, use a little *pico de gallo* or *picante* sauce instead of the tomatoes.

BANANA BREAD ROYALE

If you have a little extra time when you're serving lentil or black bean soup, or if you're in a baking mood sometime and want to make something for the freezer, Banana Bread Royale is the perfect accompaniment to these soups. A woman who was a cook at New York City's famous Schrafft's restaurants gave me the recipe, and whether it is hers or theirs, it is the best I have ever tasted. I have added "Royale" to the title because "Banana Bread" doesn't do it justice.

1	cup sugar
½	cup (1 stick) butter or margarine

2	eggs
1	teaspoon baking soda
½	cup sour cream
1	teaspoon baking powder
2	soft bananas, mashed
1	teaspoon vanilla extract
1½	cups flour

1. Preheat the oven to 350°F.
2. Cream the butter with the sugar and add the eggs one at a time.
3. Dissolve the baking soda in the sour cream, then add the baking powder, mashed bananas, and vanilla.
4. Add the sour cream and butter mixtures to the flour and bake 45 minutes in a greased loaf pan.

CHILLED TARRAGON TORTELLINI

Let's hear it for the makers of the perfect little tortellini that make the Desperate Gourmet's life so easy. They come filled with meat or cheese, both equally good. You may have to ask a store clerk where they are hidden, however. Fresh tortellini need refrigeration and I have found them in assorted places ranging from the cheese department to the fresh vegetable section of different supermarkets.

The secret to making tortellini on your own is the dressing you concoct to put on top. Here's my entry for a chilled pesto salad so good that my guests always ask if I made the tortellini myself!

You can serve this extremely versatile dish as a main-course salad piled on romaine lettuce leaves with strips of prosciutto ham and imported olives on top or on the side. You can also serve it hot or cold as a first course or a side dish.

3	to 4 tablespoons tarragon vinegar (taste after 3!)
½	cup olive oil
1	tablespoon dried tarragon
2	tablespoons freshly grated Parmesan or Romano cheese
2	10-ounce packages cheese- or meat-filled tortellini, cooked and drained
	Romaine lettuce leaves
¼	pound prosciutto or Westphalian ham, in strips
	Greek or Italian olives

1. With a wire whisk mix the vinegar into the olive oil and add the tarragon and grated cheese.
2. Toss the dressing with the tortellini and chill. When ready to serve, spoon onto the lettuce leaves and arrange the ham and olives on top or on the side.

GREEK SALAD

Served with imported Genoa salami sliced paper thin, Greek or Italian bread, and sweet butter, Greek Salad makes a lovely light supper or brunch. If you've found a good source for olives and have some on hand, so much the better. The other essential ingredient is good-quality feta cheese, which many supermarkets stock these days. If your gourmet store sells fresh feta, buy it there. If they also sell good Genoa salami, you've got it made.

Try the dressing made with lemon juice, then try it with wine vinegar. Both are authentic, according to our Greek friends, who also tell us, however, that in Greece the salads contain no lettuce at all.

½	**head romaine lettuce**
½	**cup chopped fresh parsley**
6	**green onions, sliced**
2	**tomatoes, cubed**
	Handful of Greek olives
¼	**pound feta cheese**
½	**cup olive oil**
	Juice of 2 lemons or 2 tablespoons red wine vinegar
1	**tablespoon each dried mint and oregano**
	Salt and pepper to taste

1. Tear the lettuce into bite-size pieces and toss in a salad bowl with the parsley, green onions, tomatoes, olives, and crumbled feta cheese. Cover and refrigerate.
2. Mix the oil, lemon juice or wine vinegar, mint, oregano, and salt and pepper, and set aside. When ready to serve, toss with the chilled salad.

SEAFOOD SALAD IN HIGH SPIRITS

Since the advent of the cholesterol count, dressings made with mayonnaise have been all but banished from the table. I agree that lighter, subtler dressings are more healthful and more interesting—with one exception. I love unsubtle cocktail sauce on shrimp, and I submit the following for any combination of cold seafood (even the new imitation crab or "sea legs" if the budget chooses), jazzed up by the addition of tiny amounts of several different spirits. Toss in some cold pasta if that idea appeals to you.

1   cup Miracle Whip or other mayonnaise-based salad
    dressing
½   cup cocktail sauce
½   teaspoon Dijon-style mustard
½   teaspoon Pickapeppa or Worcestershire sauce
½   teaspoon curry powder
1   teaspoon each brandy, vodka, port, and dry sherry
    Fresh lemon juice (optional)
    Salt (optional)
1   pound cooked shrimp, crab, lobster, or any
    combination

1. Mix all the sauce ingredients together, stirring in the spirits last. Taste and, if needed, add lemon juice and salt to taste.
2. Toss with the seafood and chill until ready to serve.

D. G. QUICHE LORRAINE

Years before quiches appeared on almost every lunch menu in the country, they were one of my favorite D. G. Lights. I whipped them up two at a time, once I discovered that they lost no flavor or texture when frozen and defrosted. By remembering that *all* quiches are a variation of 3 eggs to 1 cup half-and-half or 4 eggs to 1½ cups, depending on the amount of the other ingredients, plus some grated cheese, you can make successful quiches from almost anything in your refrigerator. Naturally I am very grateful for the improved quality of frozen pie shells, since Desperate Gourmets do not make pie shells.

Now that the quiche craze is fading, I am serving them again! My three favorites include two that are almost instant: a D. G. version of classic Quiche Lorraine, made with bacon, ham and Swiss cheese, and an equally quick unclassic crab quiche. The Spinach/Sausage Quiche requires a little more preparation time but is hearty enough to provide the nourishment for an entire meal and is a D. G. natural because two can be made in about the same time as one.

> **2**   strips cooked bacon, crumbled (optional)
> **1**   cup diced smoked ham
> **1**   cup diced Swiss cheese (imported or aged)
> **1**   9″ unbaked pie shell (thawed if frozen)
> **4**   eggs
> **1½**   cups half-and-half
>   Pinch ground nutmeg
>   Freshly ground pepper to taste

1. Preheat the oven to 350°F.
2. Spread the bacon, ham, and Swiss cheese inside the pie shell.
3. Beat the eggs and mix in the half-and-half, nutmeg, and pepper. Pour over the cheese mixture.
4. Bake about 45 minutes or until the custard is set and the top is lightly browned.

WIKI WIKI CRAB QUICHE

The name of this quiche may offend the French origins of the classic recipe, but it pleases my husband, who was born in Hawaii, where *wiki wiki* means "quick quick."

> **4**   ounces shredded Swiss cheese
> **1**   9″ unbaked pie shell (thawed if frozen)
> **1**   6-ounce can crabmeat (or ¾ cup fresh crab)
> **3**   green onions, sliced
> **3**   eggs
> **1**   cup half-and-half
> **½**   teaspoon each salt, dry mustard, and lemon peel
>   Pinch mace
> **¼**   cup sliced almonds

1. Preheat the oven to 325°F.
2. Sprinkle the cheese over the pie shell. Top with the crabmeat and green onions.
3. Beat the eggs and mix in all remaining ingredients except the almonds. Pour over the cheese and crab.
4. Top with the almonds and bake about 45 minutes or until set.

TWO SPINACH/SAUSAGE QUICHES

1	pound bulk sausage
4	green onions, sliced
2	teaspoons minced garlic
¾	pound fresh spinach or 1 10-ounce package frozen chopped spinach, thawed
1	cup seasoned croutons
3	cups shredded Monterey Jack cheese
2	9″ deep-dish pie shells (thawed if frozen)
6	eggs
3	cups half-and-half

1. Preheat the oven to 375°F.
2. Brown the sausage in a skillet or in a microwave oven with the green onions and garlic.
3. If using fresh spinach, wash and chop the leaves.
4. Combine the spinach, croutons, and cheese with the sausage mixture, and divide between the 2 pie shells.
5. Beat the eggs with the half-and-half and pour on top.
6. Bake 20 to 30 minutes or until set.

SALADE NIÇOISE

On a warm evening, when eating itself seems to require more energy than you can muster, this salad from southern France is a real treat. Since all the ingredients except the hard-boiled eggs are uncooked, its crisp freshness is a welcome change from soggy weather. When the salad is arranged artistically on a platter, its colorful eye appeal has an energizing effect on the weather weary. Most of its American adaptations have fewer vegetables than the original French creation—a change I wouldn't make—and substitute tuna for the traditional anchovy fillets, which suits me just fine, since I am not an anchovy fan. You're on your own there.

3	tomatoes, quartered
1	red onion, sliced
1	each red, green, and yellow peppers, sliced
1½	dozen extra-thin French green beans (*haricots verts*) or the thinnest green beans you can find
1	14-ounce can artichoke hearts
	Italian or Greek black olives

> 6   **hard-boiled eggs, quartered**
> 1   **2-ounce can anchovy fillets or 2 6½-ounce cans tuna**
>   **Vinaigrette dressing made with 3 parts olive oil to 1 part red wine vinegar, salt, pepper, and a little Dijon-style mustard *or* very fine quality (tell me I can trust you!) bottled vinaigrette**

1. With an eye for size, shape, and color, arrange all the ingredients on a large decorative platter. If using tuna instead of anchovies, try to keep it in bite-size chunks.
2. Drizzle vinaigrette over the whole platter and refrigerate until serving time.

Note: If you are sure that all partakers are anchovy lovers, mix a little anchovy paste into the vinaigrette with a wire whisk. This will approximate the authentic ground anchovies the natives of Nice call *pissalat* and spread directly on the vegetables before adding the dressing.

FALAFEL

A light supper or brunch consisting of a Middle Eastern specialty called Falafel (seasoned patties made with chick peas, bulgur wheat, and spices and served with tahini sauce) and a refreshing salad is a healthful change from meat and pasta and will wake up both the over- and the understimulated palate.

Neither recipe is hard to make once you have found a Middle Eastern grocery or health food store that carries bulgur wheat and tahini (ground sesame seeds). They may also carry a falafel mix made by Mira International Foods, which is pretty good for those really desperate moments.

Falafel can be served two ways: plain, topped with a little tahini sauce, or tucked into pita bread pockets with tahini sauce and lettuce and tomato or tomato and fresh coriander.

Falafel has two other advantages for the Desperate Gourmet: the patties can be mixed up ahead of time and sautéed at the last minute or sautéed ahead of time and reheated in the oven or the microwave. Best of all, since many people have never heard of, let alone tasted, falafel, you get high marks for introducing them to an exciting new taste.

> ¾   **cup bulgur wheat or 1 cup breadcrumbs**
> 1   **15-ounce can chick peas, drained**
> 1   **large onion, cut in half**
> 1   **egg**

> 2   teaspoons minced garlic
> 2   teaspoons ground cumin
> 2   tablespoons minced fresh parsley
> 2   tablespoons minced fresh or 2 teaspoons dried
>   mint
> 1   teaspoon salt
>   Olive oil
>   Tahini sauce (equal parts tahini and mayonnaise)
> 6   pita bread pockets (optional)
>   Lettuce, tomato, fresh coriander (optional)

1. Soak the bulgur for about 20 minutes in water to cover, then dry on paper towels. If you cannot find bulgur wheat, substitute dry bread-crumbs.
2. If you have a food processor, insert the steel knife and put into the bowl the chick peas, onion, egg, garlic, cumin, parsley, mint, and salt. If you don't have a food processor, chop the onion and parsley by hand, beat the egg, and mix them in the container of a blender along with the chick peas and spices. Process until fine.
3. Transfer to a bowl, add the soaked and dried bulgur wheat or bread-crumbs, and mix well.
4. Form the mixture into flat patties and sauté in olive oil in a heavy skillet until golden brown on each side.
5. Serve plain with tahini sauce or spread tahini sauce inside pita pockets and fill with a falafel patty, lettuce, tomato and/or coriander leaves. You can warm the pita bread first if you prefer.

LEMON-DILL DRESSING

When you're really desperate, it's great to have a terrific homemade salad dressing in your refrigerator. Armed with that, you can create a super salad from whatever rabbit food you happen to have on hand.

Two of my favorite salad dressings are Lemon-Dill and Tarragon Vinaigrette, both of which can be mixed up in a minute in any quantity you choose and will keep for at least a month in a covered jar in your refrigerator. The quality is better than any store-bought dressing on the market.

> ¼   cup olive oil
>   Juice of 2 lemons
> 1   teaspoon Dijon-style mustard
> ¼   teaspoon honey
> 1   tablespoon minced fresh or 1 teaspoon dried dill

1. Beat the olive oil into the lemon juice with a wire whisk.
2. Add the remaining ingredients and refrigerate in a covered bottle.

TARRAGON VINAIGRETTE

1	**cup olive oil**
½	**cup white wine vinegar**
1	**egg yolk**
2	**tablespoons dried tarragon**
1	**teaspoon Dijon-style mustard**
	Salt and freshly ground pepper to taste

1. Beat the olive oil slowly into the vinegar with a wire whisk.
2. Beat in the egg yolk, tarragon, mustard, and seasonings and refrigerate in a covered bottle.

WARM WILTED SPINACH

When you tire of all the variations on the theme of salad, try serving Warm Wilted Spinach with any of the main dishes in this chapter. Since it takes minutes to prepare, it's the perfect Desperate Gourmet green.

1   pound fresh spinach leaves, washed

1. Shake the excess water from the spinach leaves but do not dry.
2. Put the leaves in a saucepan over a low flame and toss them with your fingers. When they are too hot to handle, they're done!

FOR THE DRESSING   You can coat the spinach with a small amount of the above dressings or with 3 parts olive oil to 1 part rice wine vinegar mixed with a little dry mustard, crushed garlic, and salt and pepper to taste. If you have black bean sauce in the house, you can thin it with a little soy sauce, add a hint of ginger, and coat the spinach with it. Or you can just use plain soy sauce mixed with ginger.

16

THE COMPLEAT COCKTAIL PARTY: FOOD AND DRINK

FOOD FOR DRINK

Now that you've stocked the bar (see Chapter 5), what are you going to feed all those people? Certainly not intricate hot hors d'oeuvres that take all day to produce and a kitchen crew to reheat and serve.

The well-organized Desperate Gourmet with no time to plan or shop can start by raiding the pantry. In case of emergency, this resource will provide all the necessary provisions for a fine cocktail party.

One step up from pop-top hors d'oeuvres are the ones that meet two or more of the Desperate Gourmet criteria:

1. They please most of the people all of the time.
2. They can be prepared quickly and easily in a batch.

3. They can be frozen in individual serving dishes.
4. They do not lose any flavor when defrosted.
5. They can be served with a basket of crackers or bread.

HOMEMADE BOURSIN

Homemade Boursin is my rebellion against the endless hunks of cheese (usually still cold) I have been served by desperate hosts and hostesses who haven't solved their way out of the problem.

> 1½ **pounds cream cheese**
> 1 **cup sour cream**
> 1 **tablespoon minced garlic**
> 3 **tablespoons each minced fresh parsley and basil**
> **or 1 tablespoon dried basil**
> **Salt and pepper**

1. Soften the cream cheese in a microwave oven if you have one or at room temperature if you don't.
2. Blend all the ingredients in a food processor or by hand. Taste and add additional garlic and herbs if desired.
3. Fill 8 individual soufflé or other dishes with the mixture and freeze what you won't use within 2 weeks.

SHRIMP PÂTÉ

This Shrimp Pâté is a no-sacrifice find for gourmet weight and cholesterol watchers. If your fish man won't shell and devein shrimp for you, buy shelled frozen shrimp and let them defrost in a colander in the sink.

> 1 **pound cooked shrimp**
> 3 **ounces dry white wine**
> 1 **teaspoon dried tarragon**
> **Salt and freshly ground pepper to taste**
> **Juice of 1 lemon**
> **Olive oil**

1. Grind the shrimp very fine in the food processor using the metal blade.
2. Add all the other ingredients except the olive oil.

3. Slowly add enough olive oil until the mixture has the consistency of thick paste.
4. Refrigerate and/or freeze the pâté in small soufflé dishes or crocks.

SALMON MOUSSE SPREAD

Molded to perfection in the shape of a fish, this spread probably made its debut as salmon mousse at a ladies' luncheon. You'll recognize suspicious fifties ingredients like canned tomato soup and gelatin, but don't let that stop you. When I turned the mousse into an hors d'oeuvre one day, I discovered that it was delicious as a cocktail spread.

This is the basic version. Once you've tried it, you may want to vary it with herbs of your choice. The recipe fills about 8 individual soufflé dishes and freezes well.

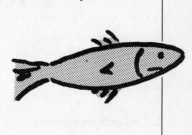

1	10¾-ounce can undiluted tomato soup
½	pound cream cheese
1	envelope plain gelatin
¼	cup very hot water
¼	large onion
1	green pepper
1	15½-ounce can salmon
	Juice of 1 lemon
6	drops Tabasco sauce
1	cup mayonnaise

1. In a microwave oven or on top of the stove, heat the soup with the cream cheese.
2. Dissolve the gelatin in the water and add the soup.
3. Chop the onion and green pepper in the food processor or by hand and add to the soup mixture. Add the salmon.
4. Add the lemon juice, Tabasco, and mayonnaise.
5. Fill individual soufflé dishes with the mixture and refrigerate and/or freeze.

BABAGANOUSH

There are many versions of this wonderful Middle Eastern eggplant specialty. Of all the ones I've tasted, I think the following is the best.

Eggplants vary in quality. If the consistency of the Babaganoush is too runny, mix in a slice of white bread soaked in vinegar. Babaganoush also makes a good salad or vegetable.

2	medium eggplants
1	small onion, peeled
¼	cup mayonnaise
2	teaspoons minced garlic
3	tablespoons olive oil
1½	tablespoons tarragon vinegar
	Oregano, salt, and pepper to taste

1. Cook the eggplants 8 minutes in a microwave or 30 minutes at 550°F or until they literally cave in. Cool.
2. Chop the onion in the food processor or by hand and add to the eggplant pulp.
3. Add all the other ingredients and blend well.
4. Refrigerate and/or freeze.

CHAMPIGNONS À LA GRECQUE

These mushrooms are another favorite with people watching their caloric intake, and since the recipe uses pure olive oil, most of which is not consumed, it is also good for people concerned about cholesterol. How does it taste? Fantastic!

2	pounds mushrooms
2	cups olive oil
2	cups dry white wine
1	teaspoon salt
¼	teaspoon white pepper
2	teaspoons curry powder
2	bay leaves
2	teaspoons minced garlic
3	tablespoons lemon juice
2	teaspoons grated lemon rind

1. Bring all ingredients to a boil and simmer 15 minutes.
2. Chill until ready to serve in a little sauce, with toothpicks.

HUMMUS

Hummus is another of the Middle Eastern wonders. Aside from its wonderful fresh taste, its "desperate" virtues are that it can be prepared on demand from ingredients right in your pantry and will keep for weeks in the refrigerator. I have tried many recipes and find most of them don't contain enough lemon juice. This one solves the problem.

Occasionally you will come across a grocery store that sells *fresh* chick peas (also called garbanzo beans) in a plastic bag in its fresh vegetable section. If you ever do, grab them! The difference in taste is amazing.

> **1 15-ounce can chick peas, drained**
> **Juice of 2 lemons**
> **2 teaspoons minced garlic**
> **1 tablespoon olive oil**
> **1 tablespoon Oriental sesame oil**
> **Seasoned salt**

1. Put all the ingredients except the salt in the bowl of a food processor or in a blender and puree.
2. Add seasoned salt to taste.
3. Chill and/or freeze before serving with crackers or raw vegetables.

• • • • • • • • • • • • • • • • • • • •

So much for the hors d'oeuvres that can be made in a batch and refrigerated or frozen. Here is my favorite collection of hors d'oeuvres that can be made in minutes the day you need them.

BUBBLY ARTICHOKE DIP

If you're looking for an artichoke dip that tastes like crabmeat, try this.

> **2 14-ounce cans artichoke hearts**
> **1 cup freshly grated Parmesan cheese**
> **1 cup mayonnaise**
> **Juice of 1 large lemon**
> **Paprika**

1. Cut the artichoke hearts into quarters.
2. Add the Parmesan cheese, mayonnaise, and lemon juice. Sprinkle with paprika.
3. Bake in an oven-to-table baking dish 5 to 8 minutes in a microwave oven on high or 20 minutes at 325°F in a standard oven.
4. Serve bubbling hot on crackers.

TZAZIKI

If you don't usually keep plain yogurt and a cucumber in the house, you'll want to start doing so after you taste this refreshing Greek hors d'oeuvre.

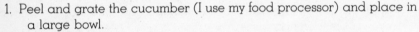

1	large cucumber
1	teaspoon sea salt
2	cups plain yogurt
	Juice of 2 lemons
2	teaspoons minced garlic
2	to 3 tablespoons minced fresh parsley
¼	cup olive oil

1. Peel and grate the cucumber (I use my food processor) and place in a large bowl.
2. Add all the remaining ingredients and stir until well blended.
3. Chill and serve with pita bread, French bread, or crackers.

"WET CONCRETE"

The following recipe comes from Caroline S. Cochran, one of Baltimore's best-loved hostesses. I love the reverse snobbery of calling a caviar dip Wet Concrete, but if you prefer, you can call it Fish Jam Spread in honor of Auntie Mame.

1	4-ounce jar lumpfish caviar
1	tablespoon lemon juice
6	drops Tabasco sauce
1	cup mayonnaise or sour cream (or a combination)

The directions for this one are really taxing: Mix together and serve with crackers for dunking.

TAG END CHEESE BALL

Tag End Cheese Ball is an ingenious way to use up all the odds and ends of good cheese that accumulate in the refrigerator. Before you label them hopeless and throw them away, try this instead. Needless to say, the taste is never the same twice.

¾ **cup cheese (any combination of varieties)**
2 **tablespoons butter**
2 **tablespoons brandy, sherry, or burgundy**
Chopped pecans or walnuts (optional)

1. Mix the cheese and butter thoroughly before adding the sherry, brandy, or burgundy. You'll have to experiment to see which flavor you prefer.
2. Pack into a crock or form into a ball and roll in chopped pecans or walnuts.

GOURMET NACHOS

No, Virginia, you don't have to make nachos with Cheese Whiz!

Spread any good-quality softened cheese (or some of the Tag End Cheese Ball from the recipe above) on tortilla chips and pop them in the microwave for a minute or two. When the cheese starts melting, they're done.

DEVILED EGGS WITH A DIFFERENCE

Deviled eggs never seem to find their way into gourmet cookbooks these days, but I think this variety is worthy of inclusion. Serve it at a cocktail party when you want something a little more substantial.

Hard-boiled eggs (you decide how many)
Mayonnaise
Dijon-style mustard
Shredded coconut
Curry powder
Chopped onion
Chopped parsley

Play with the proportions on this one after you have added just enough mayonnaise to the egg yolks to moisten them. When you're satisfied, pile the yolks back into the halved whites and decorate with a little chopped parsley (not paprika or no one will know there's a difference).

Two final entries, each a little more trouble, but definitely worth it if you have the time.

GEORGE JUE'S YUI YUEN

George Jue was the owner of Lamps of China, my favorite Chinese restaurant when I lived in San Francisco. When I did a profile on him for *San Francisco* magazine, he shared this very special recipe with me.

1	**pound butterfish fillets**
½	**pound prawns or shrimp**
½	**ounce Shiitake (dried black) mushrooms, soaked in water**
3	**green onions**
1	**egg**
1	**teaspoon water**
1	**teaspoon soy sauce**
1	**teaspoon cornstarch**

1. With the steel blade in a food processor, grind the fish, shrimp, softened mushrooms, and green onions.
2. Beat the egg with the water, soy sauce, and cornstarch and add to fish mixture until it is gooey.
3. Shape into walnut-size balls, place on a lightly oiled dish, and steam 20 to 30 minutes.
4. Serve with Chinese plum sauce or chutney.

PRESSED SALMON

Pressed Salmon is not hard to make and will really impress sushi bar addicts.

1	**bunch fresh dill, minced**
2	**tablespoons salt**
2	**tablespoons sugar**
8	**white peppercorns, crushed, or freshly ground white pepper**
1	**pound fresh salmon fillet**

1. Mix the dill, salt, sugar, and peppercorns together and line a baking dish with ⅓ of the mixture.

2. Add half the fish, another third of the mix, the other half of the fish, and the remaining mixture on top.
3. Put a heavy plate or brick on top and marinate 36 to 48 hours, turning every 6 hours.
4. Serve on thin crackers or alone, with a bit of fresh dill or a few capers on top.

"SPECIALTY OF THE HOUSE" DRINKS

"Specialties of the House," mixed ahead and ready to serve, are one of the great secrets of the serve-yourself bar. Most people are delighted to diverge from standard cocktail party fare and avoid a line at the bar.

Serve your specialties in pretty pitchers and label them clearly so you don't have to recite their contents over and over. Don't worry about using stick-on labels and felt markers. It's preferable to the nondrinker taking a swig of the Bloody Mary he thought was still a virgin.

NIGHTTIME SANGRIA

This recipe bears no resemblance to the watered-down versions served by most restaurants. It contains no canned fruit juice, sugar, or carbonated water, and bolsters its spirits with brandy and Triple Sec. If you find it tastes too strong, try it without the brandy.

1 bottle burgundy
3 ounces brandy
3 ounces Triple Sec
Orange juice to taste
1 orange, sliced
1 lemon, sliced
1 apple, sliced

Mix the wine, brandy, and Triple Sec. Taste often as you add orange juice a little at a time. When the taste pleases you, it's right! Pour into a pitcher and add the fruit. Chill thoroughly.

To serve sangria authentically, pour it into a hand-painted pottery pitcher and add a wooden spoon for the fruit.

DANISH MARY À LA ALFRED

For decades my uncle Alfred Lowenherz has delighted the palates of his guests with his Danish Marys. Unfortunately for him, everyone is so enamored of these drinks that whenever he might prefer to pour a simple glass of wine, he is invariably begged for one of his masterpieces. I have never known him to refuse.

This recipe makes four drinks. It won't be enough.

1 lime, cut in quarters
8 dashes (approximately) Outerbridge's Sherry Pepper sauce or Pickapeppa sauce (or Tabasco as a last resort)
6 ounces aquavit (Aalborg is the best brand)
1 quart Mott's Clamato juice

Squeeze the lime quarters into a pitcher and put in the rind as well. Add the pepper sauce, aquavit, and Clamato juice. Chill. Serve on the rocks with a bit of lime in each glass.

REAL HAWAIIAN MAI TAIS

Never trust a Mai Tai that comes from a bottle. When we lived in Hawaii, we tasted many wonderful versions of this island specialty, and this is the one our mainland party guests love. If you serve it in a punch bowl, float pineapple spears on top. If it's really a gala, float gardenias or orchids instead.

This recipe makes 20 drinks.

½ quart light rum
5 ounces curaçao liqueur
1 quart orange juice
1 quart pineapple juice
Juice of 6 lemons
½ quart dark rum

Mix together all but the dark rum and pour into a pitcher or punch bowl. Float the dark rum on top. Add ice and keep chilled until ready to serve.

"EPISCOPAL PUNCH"

This exquisitely simple southern specialty was renamed by one of our houseguests on the grounds of the Bay View Music Festival. Originally created as a summer camp for Methodist ministers, Bay View still maintains an official "no alcohol on the grounds" policy. So our guest's self proclaimed Episcopal mission was to produce a festive drink that *looked* innocent. If this beautifully colored concoction ever had a proper name, it has since been lost. Call it what you will, it's a great addition to a party!

Mix equal parts of sweet and dry vermouth in a glass pitcher (glass because the color is so lovely), chill well, and serve in stem glasses without ice.

MAY WINE PUNCH

This authentic German import has nothing in common with the usual sauterne-and-soda punches we would be happy never to meet again.

- **4**   **bottles German Riesling wine**
- **1**   **bottle champagne**
- **2**   **ounces Benedictine liqueur**
- **4**   **ounces brandy**
- **¼**   **pound superfine sugar**
- **1**   **pint sparkling water**
- **1**   **pint fresh strawberries, hulled**

In a punch bowl, mix the chilled wine and champagne with the Benedictine and brandy. Dissolve the sugar in the sparkling water and stir in. Add the strawberries. If you want the punch to stay really cold without diluting, mound shaved ice in the center of the punch bowl.

PIQUANT MULLED TEA

So many people are avoiding alcohol these days, it isn't fair to relegate them to soda and fruit juice, especially in winter when the other guests are happily sipping mulled wine. Piquant mulled tea is a delicious non-alcoholic alternative.

- **1**   **cup honey**
- **1**   **cup water**

> 1½ **tablespoons each grated orange and lemon rind**
> 2   **cinnamon sticks**
>   **Dash each ground cloves and allspice**
> 12 **cups orange- or lemon-flavored tea**
>   **Cider (optional)**

Boil the honey, water, rind, and spices 5 minutes or until the honey dissolves. Add the steeped tea. Taste and add cider as desired. Serve hot.

ANGLO-SWEDISH GLÖGG

Traditional Swedish glögg is a warm, heady mixture of wines and spices with aquavit, which elevates it to a lofty realm. To me, the traditional recipes have far too much sugar. As for the addition of raisins and blanched almonds, not only can I do without them at the bottom of my glass, you'll never find blanching almonds on any D. G.—approved activity list.

All I can say about Anglo-Swedish Glögg is it seems to leave all other beverages in the dust at parties. Since people have different preferences about the amount of aquavit they like in glögg, starting with none, we find it best to put the bottle of aquavit on the side and let guests add their own.

> 2   **quarts dry red wine**
> 2   **quarts muscatel**
> 1   **pint sweet vermouth**
> 2   **teaspoons dried orange peel or the peel from a**
>   **fresh orange**
> 1   **teaspoon ground cardamom**
> ½   **teaspoon ground cloves**
> ½   **teaspoon ground ginger**
> ½   **cup sugar**
> 1   **bottle aquavit**

1. In a large casserole that can double as a serving vessel or in any large pot, mix all the ingredients except the aquavit and heat gently about 20 minutes.
2. Let cool if not serving immediately and reheat before serving. If heated in a pot, transfer the glögg to a punch bowl and try to keep it warm while serving (a small electric heating square is ideal for this purpose). Serve the aquavit on the side and let guests add it themselves.

· 17 ·

D.G. DINNERS FOR EIGHT, COMPLETE WITH SHOPPING LISTS

· · · · · · · · · · · · · · · · · · · ·

MOST of my overextended friends tell me they don't entertain at home as often as they'd like because it's too time-consuming to plan a menu, check the ingredients, make a shopping list from the different recipes, and then do all the shopping and cooking. For this reason, I have simplified the process not only by offering complete menus that have received rave reviews from all our guests, but by offering the shopping list for each menu as well.

Each shopping list is divided into two parts: first, the ingredients I assume you have in your basic pantry, and second, the ingredients I assume you will have to go out and buy for the occasion. Check the first list carefully. If your basic pantry is missing one or two items,

---

simply add them to the shopping list. The shopping lists are not designed to be autocratic. If you don't like one of the recipes in the menu, simply scratch the ingredients from the list and substitute something of your own. If you decide to substitute a precooked or store-bought item for one of the recipes, simply omit those ingredients from the shopping list and proceed.

Each menu is composed of flavors and textures that were designed to complement one another, so if you substitute, try to replace the item with something of a similarly light or heavy consistency, strong or delicate flavor, smooth or crunchy texture. Each recipe was chosen for its sophisticated taste and simplicity of preparation, following the most basic Desperate Gourmet principle: Let your guests think you spent all day in the kitchen just for them when in reality you haven't spent more than an hour.

Don't be concerned if the menus take a little longer than an hour to prepare at first. Remember the Desperate Gourmet's motto for successful entertaining:

Keep it simple, make it special, serve it often enough not to have to think about it.

Also remember the second most important Desperate Gourmet principle:

If you think your guests might get sacrificed to the menu, simplify it.

None of these dinners starts with a first course because it's next to impossible to prepare an entire dinner *plus* a first course in an hour or less, and it's absolutely impossible to serve a sit-down buffet that starts with a first course. When I have the help to serve a formal sit-down dinner, that's a different story, but at that point you can add your own. I usually choose several hors d'oeuvres from Chapter 16 and serve those with drinks instead of a first course.

Note: The recipes are printed in the order in which they should be prepared for greatest efficiency.

▪ MENU 1 ▪

Indonesian Spicy Beef
Oven-Fried Rice
Spinach Salad with Lemon-Dill Dressing
Intoxicated Mud Pie (page 139)

● ● ● ● ● ● ● ● ● ● ● ● ● ● ● ● ● ● ●

From Your Pantry

Rice, bay leaves, ground red pepper, dried mint, dill weed or dill salt, caraway seeds, ground coriander, olive oil, peanut oil, Dijon-style mustard, chicken bouillon cubes, honey, brown sugar, brandy, chopped garlic in oil or fresh garlic.

Shopping List

2 pounds sirloin or other tender beef (ask the butcher to cut into 1½″ × 1″ strips if possible)
3 onions
1 pint cherry tomatoes
2 limes
2 lemons
1½ pounds fresh spinach or 2 10-ounce packages frozen leaf spinach
1 chocolate cookie crumb pie shell
1 quart coffee ice cream (or other flavor if you hate coffee)
   Fudge sauce (ordinary chocolate won't do)

OVEN-FRIED RICE
● ●

1 **large onion, chopped**
2 **cups long-grain rice**
¼ **cup vegetable oil**
2 **teaspoons minced garlic**
2 **tablespoons dried mint**
6 **chicken bouillon cubes**

1. Preheat the oven to 325°F.
2. In a large skillet, sauté the onion and rice lightly in the oil, then add the garlic and mint. Transfer to a casserole.
3. Boil 2½ cups water and dissolve the bouillon cubes in it. Add to the casserole.
4. Bake, covered, for 1 hour. Uncover and bake 10 minutes longer.

SPINACH SALAD WITH LEMON-DILL DRESSING

1½	pounds fresh spinach or 2 10-ounce packages frozen leaf spinach, thawed
1	pint cherry tomatoes
	Lemon-Dill Dressing (page 75)

INDONESIAN SPICY BEEF

1	large onion, chopped
2	teaspoons minced garlic
3	tablespoons peanut oil
2	tablespoons brown sugar
	Juice of 2 limes
2	bay leaves
1½	teaspoons each ground coriander and caraway seeds
	Salt and pepper to taste
2	pounds sirloin or tender beef, cut in 1½" × 1" strips

1. Lightly sauté the onion and garlic in the oil.
2. Add all the other ingredients except the beef and stir just to combine.
3. Add the beef and cook not longer than a minute or 2.

That's it—a very easy, anything-but-ordinary dinner you can create in about 10 minutes in the grocery store and about 45 minutes in the kitchen.

If making four recipes from scratch is still too much trouble:

- substitute plain rice for oven-fried rice *or*
- let the deli section of the grocery store make your salad (as long as it's really fresh) *or*

- keep the lemon-dill dressing already mixed up in your refrigerator *or*
- always keep an extra mud pie in your freezer and roll it out at times like this.

▪ MENU 2 ▪

Imperial Crab
Peas with Fresh Coriander
Fruited Rice
Almost Instant Pecan Pie (page 142)

From Your Pantry

Butter, rice, sugar, dark corn syrup, vanilla, Dijon-style mustard, ground cumin, chopped garlic in oil or fresh garlic, chicken bouillon cubes, eggs, mayonnaise, Worcestershire sauce

Shopping List

2	pounds fresh or frozen crabmeat
2	green peppers
1	bunch fresh parsley
1	head red leaf or romaine lettuce
1	bunch fresh coriander, dill, or parsley
1	1-pound bag frozen green peas
1	large bag broken pecans
1	red onion
1	frozen pie shell
1	8-ounce bag mixed dried fruit

IMPERIAL CRAB

If you take the trouble to track down top-quality crabmeat (back fin or claw meat, either fresh or frozen), this will probably become one of the easiest and most elegant recipes in your repertoire.

6 tablespoons mayonnaise
1 teaspoon Worcestershire or Pickapeppa sauce

1 teaspoon Dijon-style mustard
2 green peppers, minced
1 bunch fresh parsley, chopped not too fine
2 eggs
Salt and white pepper to taste
2 pounds fresh crabmeat

1. Preheat the oven to 325°F.
2. Mix together all the ingredients except the crabmeat.
3. Pick over crabmeat for shell remnants, being careful not to break it into smaller pieces, and add it carefully to the mixture.
4. Bake 20 to 30 minutes.

FRUITED RICE

2 cups long-grain rice
4 chicken bouillon cubes
4 cups water
½ cup mixed dried fruit, minced

1. Put all the ingredients in a saucepan and bring to a boil.
2. Cover and cook about 20 minutes or until done.

PEAS WITH FRESH CORIANDER

1 1-pound bag frozen green peas, thawed
1 teaspoon minced garlic
⅓ to ½ red onion
½ bunch fresh coriander, dill, or parsley
2 tablespoons lemon juice
1 teaspoon ground cumin
1 teaspoon salt or to taste
Large lettuce leaves

1. Place all the ingredients except the lettuce leaves in the bowl of a food processor fitted with the metal blade. Grind until well blended.
2. Line a pretty platter with the lettuce leaves and mound the peas on top. Refrigerate until serving time.

▪ MENU 3 ▪

Shoyu Chicken
White Rice
Stir-Fried Broccoli
Quick Pots de Crème (page 138)

• • • • • • • • • • • • • • • • • •

From Your Pantry

Sugar, fresh or ground ginger, chopped garlic in oil or fresh garlic, rice, peanut oil, soy sauce, eggs, dark rum, sherry

Shopping List

8 chicken breasts (or 4 leg and 4 breast quarters)
1 head broccoli
1 bunch fresh basil, mint, or dill
1 quart whole milk (this is a substitute for cream, so don't use low-fat or skim milk)
1 12-ounce package semisweet chocolate chips (read the label; there's a lot of imitation chocolate out there)

SHOYU CHICKEN

• •

1 **cup sugar**
2 **cups soy sauce**
⅔ **cup sherry**
2 **teaspoons shredded fresh ginger or 1 teaspoon ground ginger**
2 **teaspoons minced garlic**
8 **whole chicken breasts (or 4 leg and breast quarters)**

1. Mix together all the ingredients except the chicken, pour over the chicken, and marinate at least 2 hours (12 to 24 hours is even better).
2. Preheat the oven to 325°F.

3. Place the chicken, skin side down, in a large baking pan and bake about 1 hour.

4. Turn the chicken over for an additional ½ hour of baking.

Note: If the sauce is too thin, dissolve about 1 tablespoon cornstarch in a little hot sauce and add to the rest, stirring until well blended.

WHITE RICE

While the chicken is cooking, cook about 2 cups long-grain white rice. Add chopped parsley for color just before serving. Serve the sauce from the chicken in a gravy boat or let people spoon it over the rice from the dish the chicken is served in.

STIR-FRIED BROCCOLI

This is the basic recipe. Experiment with it! Add feta cheese and oregano and omit the soy sauce for a Greek flavor. Sauté it in olive oil and add lemon juice and sun-dried tomatoes for an Italian twist.

1	**head broccoli**
4	**to 6 tablespoons peanut oil**
1	**to 2 teaspoons minced garlic**
¼	**cup soy sauce**
3	**to 4 tablespoons minced fresh herbs**

1. Peel the ends of the broccoli and slice into bite-size rounds. Cut the flowers into a manageable size for eating without a knife.

2. In a wok or heavy skillet, heat the oil until very hot and sauté the broccoli stems 3 to 4 minutes. Add the flowers and sauté an additional minute or 2.

3. Add the garlic, soy sauce, and herbs and heat through.

▪ MENU 4 ▪

**Rack of Lamb Marsala with New
  Potatoes
Gingered Snow Peas
Strawberries in Champagne (page 137)
Cookies (from Chapter 19 or your local
  bakery)**

• • • • • • • • • • • • • • • • •

From Your Pantry

Marsala wine, chopped garlic in oil or fresh garlic, thyme, marjoram, bay leaves, soy sauce with or without ginger, vegetable oil, sugar

Shopping List

    Rack of lamb (or 8 lamb chops)
1   dozen tiny new potatoes
1   pound snow peas
1   bunch fresh parsley
1   bunch fresh mint
1   head celery
2   quarts fresh strawberries
1   bottle champagne

RACK OF LAMB MARSALA
WITH NEW POTATOES

• •

    **Rack of lamb or 8 thick rib lamb chops, ½ to ¾
  pound each**
2   **teaspoons minced garlic
Dried thyme and marjoram to taste
Minced fresh parsley to taste
Freshly ground pepper to taste
Vegetable oil for searing
Salt to taste**
1½ **cups Marsala wine**

97

1	**bay leaf**
2	**sprigs celery leaves**
	Handful minced fresh mint or 2 teaspoons dried mint
12	**tiny new potatoes, scrubbed**

1. Preheat the oven to 350°F.
2. Rub the lamb with the garlic, thyme, marjoram, parsley, and freshly ground pepper.
3. In a heavy casserole, sear the lamb in a little oil until nicely browned. Add salt to taste.
4. Add the Marsala wine, bay leaf, celery leaves, mint, and potatoes and bake 45 minutes.
5. Skim the fat before serving. Garnish the lamb with mint sprigs and pass the sauce in a separate dish.

GINGERED SNOW PEAS

1	**pound snow peas**
2	**tablespoons vegetable oil**
2	**tablespoons gingered soy sauce (or regular soy sauce with 1 teaspoon ground ginger mixed in)**

1. Cut off the stems of the pea pods with a small knife.
2. Bring several quarts of water to a boil and drop in the pea pods. When the water comes to a second boil, turn off the heat and let stand a minute or 2. Drain.
3. Add the oil and gingered soy sauce and chill. Serve on a nicely decorated flat dish.

▪ MENU 5 ▪

Salmon Lake Geneva
Wilted Spinach with *Shiitake* Mushrooms
French Bread with Anchovy-Garlic Butter
Mini Mansions' Lemon Chess Pie (page 143)

This is an ideal menu if all you have time to do before guests arrive is make a quick trip to the grocery store. The first three recipes can be made in minutes, and even the home-baked pie can be mixed up in no time and baked while you are dining. If your local grocery doesn't have dried mushrooms and you're too rushed to make an extra stop, substitute broken cashews or chopped walnuts.

From Your Pantry
Flour, cornmeal, sugar, butter, dried basil, peanut oil, soy sauce, cornstarch, chopped garlic in oil or fresh garlic, sherry, dry white wine

Shopping List
8   salmon fillets (about 3 pounds), ½" thick
1½ pounds fresh spinach
1½ -ounce package dried *shiitake* mushrooms
2   large onions
3   lemons
    French or Italian bread (try to find the real thing with a hard crust and soft inside)
    Anchovy paste if it isn't in your pantry

SALMON LAKE GENEVA

8   **salmon steaks (about 3 pounds), ¾" thick**
    Salt and freshly ground pepper
    Dried basil
    Flour
6   **tablespoons (¾ stick) butter**
2   **onions**
    Dry white wine

1. Rub both sides of the salmon fillets with salt, pepper, basil, and flour.
2. Heat the butter in a large skillet and sauté the salmon quickly on both sides or until the fish starts to pull away from the bone. Remove the fillets and keep warm. (You can do this in the microwave.)
3. Shred the onions and sauté them in the same butter. When golden, spread them over the fish.
4. Add a little wine to the remaining butter in the pan and pour over the fish and onions.

WILTED SPINACH WITH *SHIITAKE* MUSHROOMS

1½	ounces dried *shiitake* mushrooms
¼	cup peanut oil
5	tablespoons soy sauce
2	tablespoons sherry
1	tablespoon sugar
1½	pounds fresh spinach

1. Break the mushrooms, put them in a small bowl, and cover with boiling water. Let stand until soft.
2. Sauté the mushroom pieces in peanut oil, then add all the remaining ingredients except the spinach and blend.
3. Wash the spinach leaves, then put them in a deep pot with only the water remaining on the leaves. Over a medium flame, heat them only until they are wilted, not cooked. Turn off the flame and toss with the sauce.

FRENCH BREAD WITH ANCHOVY-GARLIC BUTTER

French bread
Anchovy paste
Soft butter
Minced garlic

1. Cut the bread into slices but leave them attached at the bottom.
2. Mix whatever proportion of anchovy paste, butter, and minced garlic appeals to you and spread one side of each slice of bread with the mixture.
3. Heat in a slow oven until barely warm.

▪ MENU 6 ▪

Pork Chops in Plum Rum Sauce
Spartan Caesar Salad
Orzo
Grapes Brûlée

• • • • • • • • • • • • • • • • • • • •

Preparation time for this whole menu shouldn't be more than about 20 minutes if you assemble your salad and dessert ingredients while the pork is browning. Not bad for an unusual meal made entirely "from scratch."

From Your Pantry

Flour, dark brown sugar, sage, ground cinnamon, ground cloves, chopped garlic in oil or fresh garlic, Worcestershire or Pickapeppa sauce, olive oil, wine vinegar, brandy or cognac, rum

Shopping List

8   ½- to ¾-pound loin pork chops
2   4½-ounce jars strained plums (baby food)
1   6-ounce box seasoned croutons
1   1-pound package orzo or 1 pound small, shaped pasta plus 1 can artichoke hearts if you can't find orzo
1½ ounces Parmesan cheese (or more)
1   pint sour cream
2   pounds green grapes
2   lemons
3   heads romaine lettuce

PORK CHOPS IN PLUM RUM SAUCE

8	loin pork chops
	Salt and pepper
	Pinch of dried sage
2	large (7½ ounces) jars strained plums
½	cup rum
2	teaspoons grated lemon rind
1	teaspoon ground cinnamon
½	teaspoon ground cloves

1. Preheat the oven to 325°F.
2. Season the pork chops with salt and pepper, then brown in a casserole on top of the stove.
3. Mix the remaining ingredients together, pour over the chops, and bake 1 hour.

SPARTAN CAESAR SALAD

This Caesar is named for the omission of anchovies and raw egg.

1	teaspoon minced garlic
⅔	cup olive oil
1	tablespoon Pickapeppa or Worcestershire sauce
	Juice of 2 lemons
2	tablespoons wine vinegar
1	teaspoon salt
	Freshly ground pepper to taste
3	heads romaine lettuce
½	cup freshly grated Parmesan cheese
1	cup seasoned croutons

1. With a wire whisk, mix the garlic, oil, Pickapeppa sauce, lemon juice, wine vinegar, salt, and pepper. Let stand.
2. Wash the lettuce leaves and tear into bite-size pieces.
3. Just before serving, toss the lettuce with the dressing, cheese, and croutons.

ORZO

Orzo is simply Greek macaroni, but its taste and texture are above average. Since many people have never eaten it, you'll score points for originality. If you don't have a Middle Eastern grocery store near you, buy the grocery store variety made by Ronzoni. Add the herbs of your choice just before serving.

If you can't find any brand of orzo, substitute small pasta in the most appealing shape you can find at the store. Drain a can of artichoke hearts, sauté them lightly in olive oil and whatever herbs appeal to you, and add to the cooked macaroni.

GRAPES BRÛLÉE

2 **cups sour cream**
¼ **cup dark brown sugar**
3 **tablespoons cognac**
2 **pounds seedless grapes**

1. In an attractive baking dish (I use a decorated soufflé dish), mix the sour cream, brown sugar, and cognac.
2. Fold in the grapes and chill several hours.
3. Just before serving, cover the dish with additional brown sugar and put under the broiler until the top begins to caramelize. Spoon into individual dessert dishes.

▪ MENU 7 ▪

D. G. Chicken "Oscar" with Asparagus Tips
Brandied Carrots
Gingered Rice
Irish Coffee with Cookies You Didn't
Bake

From Your Pantry

Rice, white and brown sugar, butter, eggs, fresh or ground ginger, chopped garlic in oil or fresh garlic, bay leaves, tarragon, tarragon vinegar, brandy

Shopping List

3 pounds boneless chicken breasts
1 pound asparagus (the thinner the better)
1 bunch parsley
4 shallots (or 1 onion to mix with garlic, if you can't find shallots)
2 1-pound bags frozen baby carrots
½ pint cream
   Irish whiskey
   Bakery cookies (unless you have your own in the freezer)

D. G. CHICKEN "OSCAR" WITH ASPARAGUS TIPS

The original Veal Oscar, topped with sautéed crab legs, was the creation of Ernie's restaurant in San Francisco. The D. G. version can be made with boneless chicken or turkey breast and cooked in the microwave in about 2 minutes. Directions for both methods of cooking are included.

4 **shallots or 1 small onion plus 2 teaspoons minced garlic**
2 **tablespoons tarragon vinegar**
1 **teaspoon dried tarragon**
  Salt
  Freshly ground pepper
3 **egg yolks**
1 **cup (2 sticks) butter, melted**
8 **chicken breasts (halved if large), skinned and boned**
1 **pound fresh asparagus**

1. Peel and chop the shallots (or mix 2 teaspoons minced garlic with 1 chopped onion); add the tarragon vinegar and dried tarragon, salt, and pepper to taste.
2. Cook 2 minutes in the microwave or on top of the stove, or until most of the liquid has evaporated. Add the egg yolks one at a time with

a wire whisk. (Heat 1 minute after each addition if using the microwave.) Add the melted butter last.

3. In a large skillet, sauté the chicken breasts in butter several minutes or until completely white. Meanwhile, cook the asparagus in a dish covered with plastic wrap in the microwave or steam them for 3 minutes on top of the stove.

4. To serve, arrange the chicken breasts on a platter, top with the asparagus, and pour the sauce over the top.

BRANDIED CARROTS

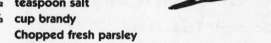

2	1-pound bags frozen baby carrots
½	cup (1 stick) butter, melted
2	tablespoons sugar
½	teaspoon salt
⅓	cup brandy
	Chopped fresh parsley

1. Cook the carrots until just tender.
2. Pour the melted butter over the carrots and add the sugar, salt, and brandy. Add the parsley just before serving.

GINGERED RICE

2	cups long-grain rice
4	teaspoons minced garlic
2	bay leaves
2	teaspoons salt
1	tablespoon shredded fresh ginger or 1 teaspoon ground ginger

1. Bring the rice to a boil in 3 cups water. Add the garlic, bay leaves, salt, and ginger.
2. Cover, reduce the heat, and simmer until all the water is absorbed.

IRISH COFFEE

Don't run out and buy special Irish Whiskey glasses or china coffee cups with shamrocks on them. Use what you have, whether it's heavy glass goblets, demitasse coffee cups, or china mugs.

An amusing note: The very Irish owner of my very favorite Irish pub swears that American rye whiskey makes the best Irish coffee.

> **Demerara or dark brown sugar**
> **5 cups very hot coffee (I use espresso, but you can use something less potent, even brewed decaf)**
> **2½ cups Irish whiskey**
> **Heavy cream**

1. Fill the glasses or cups with boiling water to heat them and pour it out just before serving.
2. Put 1 teaspoon sugar in each glass, then fill ⅔ full with hot coffee, the remaining ⅓ with whiskey, and float cream on top.

▪ MENU 8 ▪

"Gourmet" Texas Chili
Polenta
Frijoles (Mexican-Style Beans)
Figs with Coffee Cream

• • • • • • • • • • • • • • • • • •

From Your Pantry

Chopped garlic in oil or fresh garlic, chili powder, ground cumin, bay leaves, oregano, ketchup (you'll need 16 ounces; transfer to your shopping list if you don't have enough), honey, butter, Kahlua or crème de cacao

Shopping List

4   pounds ground beef
1   6-ounce can tomato paste
12 ounces (1 can) beer
1   1-pound package dried pinto or kidney beans
    Yellow cornmeal
3   large onions
1   green pepper
2   17-ounce jars whole figs or 2 16½-ounce cans blackberries
3   ounces Parmesan cheese

8   ounces sour cream
     Canned jalapeño peppers (optional)

"GOURMET" TEXAS CHILI

"Gourmet" chili is something of a contradiction in terms, but if there were such a thing, Texas Chili would win first prize. It is also one of the few cooked foods I keep in my freezer because it doesn't lose anything in the translation. Once made, it will either feed a mob once or a family of four on three different occasions, especially if frozen in separate containers.

2	large onions
1	green pepper
4	pounds ground beef
2	teaspoons minced garlic
½	teaspoon minced jalapeño pepper
½	cup chili powder
1	tablespoon ground cumin
2	bay leaves
	Salt and freshly ground pepper to taste
1	6-ounce can tomato paste
2	cups ketchup
2	tablespoons honey
12	oz. beer

1. Preheat the oven to 300°F.
2. Chop the onion and green pepper and brown with the beef and garlic in a large casserole.
3. Mix and add all the remaining ingredients and bake, uncovered, for 3 hours.

POLENTA

2	cups yellow cornmeal
4	cups cold water
2	teaspoons salt
½	cup (1 stick) butter, cut into pieces
1	cup freshly grated Parmesan cheese
	Freshly ground pepper to taste

1. Mix the cornmeal with 2 cups of the cold water and set aside.
2. Boil the other 2 cups water with the salt in a casserole you can bring

to the table. Add the cornmeal, bring it to a boil, and simmer 15 minutes.

3. To serve, toss in the butter and add the Parmesan cheese and pepper to taste.

FRIJOLES
(Mexican-Style Beans)

1   **pound dried pinto or kidney beans**
2   **whole onions, sliced**
2   **teaspoons minced garlic**
2   **teaspoons dried oregano**
    Salt to taste

1. Soak the beans in water to cover overnight.
2. Drain the beans and put them in a flameproof casserole or saucepan and add enough water to cover.
3. Add the onions, garlic, and oregano and simmer 1 hour. Salt to taste and continue cooking until tender.

FIGS WITH COFFEE CREAM

For variety, substitute Oregon brand canned blackberries for the figs. The combination of colors is beautiful.

2   **17-ounce jars whole figs**
1   **cup sour cream**
½   **cup Kahlua (or crème de cacao)**

1. Drain the figs and divide them among 8 dessert dishes or wineglasses.
2. Mix the sour cream with the Kahlua and pour over the fruit. Refrigerate in summer; serve room temperature in winter.

· 18 ·

HOT AND COLD RUNNING BUFFETS

● ● ● ● ● ● ● ● ● ● ● ● ● ● ● ● ● ●

I was recently invited to a buffet luncheon at a house in which the furnishings would rival the collection of any number of museums. The table was laid to perfection with antique china, crystal, and silver, and I who love beautiful things found myself wishing I were seated in the kitchen!

There were many more people than chairs, and the food was delicious but impossible to eat with a fork. As I stood trying to carry on a conversation, the better part of my attention was diverted to the task of trying to cut oversize pieces of lettuce and chicken (both putting up resistance) without shooting them across the plate and onto the priceless Oriental. Since everyone else was similarly preoccupied, the general level of conversation reached an all-time low. Buffet abuse, it would seem, is not limited to any particular socioeconomic group.

Fortunately, this is easily fixed. There are too many interesting "fork foods" out there for a guest to have to do battle with the buffet.

From the Desperate Gourmet's point of view, successful buffet food is the kind that can be fixed and forgotten. The last thing you need is temperamental food that falls apart when ignored. What you want is food that is independent enough to get through the evening on its own once the cook has brought it into the world. If it has to sit around on a warming tray for several hours, so be it. That's just "doin' a what comes naturally" at a buffet.

What follows are our ten most popular buffet menus, both from the host's *and* the guest's point of view. The main course recipes come with suggested side dishes and desserts, but feel free to substitute some of your own favorite fork food. A buffet dinner is the perfect occasion to incorporate a little international flair into the menu, which adds atmosphere to an evening without additional work.

The recipes in this section include all sorts of D. G. shortcuts, but they do take a little longer to prepare than some of the others. My theory is that people invite more guests than usual to a buffet, and it is not unreasonable to expect to spend a little extra preparation time.

▪ HAWAIIAN CURRY WITH ▪ ALL THE CONDIMENTS ▪

Authentic Hawaiian Curry D. G.
White rice
Condiments: shredded coconut,
**   chopped peanuts, chopped green on-**
**   ion, chutney, raisins, bacon bits**
Pineapple Pickle and/or
Bananas Flambé (see page 144)
Green Salad with Rice Vinegar Dressing
Coconut-Macadamia Ice Cream Balls

Unlike Indian curry, Hawaiian Curry is sweet and mild because it is made with coconut milk. (Don't worry, I'll tell you how to fake it if you don't live near a coconut tree.) Usually it is made with chicken or shrimp, but I use boned turkey breast for obvious D. G. reasons. If you don't mind the expense you can use flash-frozen shrimp, as long as you check for possible allergies ahead of time.

Making *Hawaiian Curry* the old-fashioned way is an all-day

affair, but when we lived in Hawaii I was motivated to create a D. G. version. Together with all the condiments—raisins, chopped peanuts, crumbled bacon, coconut, scallions—it looks beautiful on the buffet table and turns an ordinary dinner into a feast.

The non–D. G. version of this recipe is very authentic and comes from Mrs. Fritz Hart, who is one of the island's most gracious hostesses. She is the widow of the founder and conductor of the Honolulu Symphony, who inspired my husband to become a conductor at the ripe old age of five.

AUTHENTIC HAWAIIAN CURRY D. G.

If you make the curry the day before, the flavor will really penetrate the turkey. While we're on the subject of flavor, homemade curry powder is really best and very easy to mix up by using equal proportions of turmeric, ground coriander, ground cardamom, and chili pepper. If you want it a little less potent, also include paprika.

6-	to 7-pound fresh or frozen turkey breast
	Salt and pepper
3	onions, sliced
2	teaspoons minced garlic
1	teaspoon ground ginger
4	heaping teaspoons good-quality curry powder
⅓	cup flour
1	16-ounce can coconut cream (the kind for piña coladas)
1	quart whole milk

1. Cook the turkey breast (thawed if frozen) in water to cover with salt and pepper and sliced onions. Remove the turkey and, when cool enough to handle, cut into bite-size pieces. Save the broth.
2. In a blender, food processor, or mixer, puree the onions, garlic, ginger, curry powder, flour, and 1 cup of the turkey broth.
3. Add another 3 cups broth, the coconut cream, and milk and cook in the microwave oven or on top of the stove until thickened.
4. Add the turkey and set aside.

CONDIMENTS

The condiments for Hawaiian Curry should be set out in separate small dishes (unless you have a decorative dish with compartments), each with its individual spoon. If your guests have never eaten Hawaiian Curry before, you may have to tell them that the curry goes directly over the rice and a bit of each condiment goes directly on the curry.

Use imitation bacon bits if you don't want to cook and crumble real bacon. Use unsweetened coconut if you can find it, and raisins just the way they come out of the box. You will have to chop the peanuts (I assume you will let a machine do the dirty work) and cut the green onion in small pieces. Buy Major Grey's chutney and chop the large pieces.

PINEAPPLE PICKLE

1	cup brown sugar
1	cup white sugar
4	sticks of cinnamon
1	teaspoon whole cloves
¾	cup cider vinegar
1	20-ounce can pineapple chunks

1. Combine the sugars, spices, and vinegar and heat just to dissolve.
2. Place the fruit in the syrup and cook over low heat 15 minutes.

GREEN SALAD WITH RICE VINEGAR DRESSING

½	cup olive oil
½	cup vegetable oil
¼	cup rice vinegar
	Pinch dry mustard
½	teaspoon minced garlic
	Salt and pepper to taste

Use this dressing on a combination of whatever greens look freshest the day you go to the market.

COCONUT-MACADAMIA ICE CREAM BALLS

You can make these up to a week ahead. Use an ice cream scoop to make balls out of a half gallon of first-quality vanilla ice cream and roll the balls in a mixture of chopped macadamia nuts and coconut. Keep the balls covered in the freezer in whatever large ceramic bowl you will serve them in. Let guests help themselves to a fruit topping if you want to liven things up.

▪ MOUSSAKA AND OTHER ▪ GREEK DELIGHTS

Tzaziki (page 82)
Moussaka
Greek Salad (page 70)
Orzo (page 103)
Athenian Walnut Cake (page 143)

• • • • • • • • • • • • • • • • • •

Moussaka (put the accent on the final "a" if you want to pronounce it properly), a Greek casserole made of eggplant, ground lamb or beef, and a wonderful custard topping, is fine buffet fare because it is different and delicious and does very well when kept at serving temperature for a long time. It is also a good thing to serve when your guest list contains a larger than usual number of meat-and-potatoes types. Its flavor and texture are very hearty.

When we lived within easy driving distance of the thriving Greek neighborhoods in both East Baltimore and Astoria, Queens, I had occasion to sample many first-rate moussakas and try to re-create my favorites at home. It took me a while to figure out how to get the custard to stay on top instead of sinking to the middle, as it will if the cook is not in control—a trick I am happy to pass on.

Don't be scared away by the longer-than-average list of ingredients; not one is the least bit exotic. Moussaka is very easy to assemble and will feed a large crowd today or tomorrow.

MOUSSAKA
• •

Moussaka does very well made the day before and reheated. It can be served either hot or at room temperature, which makes it an ideal buffet food. Once the custard is set, it is not fragile and will not disintegrate when reheated.

| 1 | large or 2 medium eggplants |
| 1½ | pounds ground beef |

1	large or 2 medium onions, sliced
1	6-ounce can tomato paste
¾	cup red wine
2	teaspoons minced garlic
2	teaspoons dried oregano
	Salt and pepper to taste

CREAM SAUCE

¼	cup (½ stick) butter
6	tablespoons flour
3	cups milk
5	eggs
1	teaspoon salt
¾	cup freshly grated Parmesan cheese

1. Preheat the oven to 375°F.
2. Cut the eggplant into ¾" slices and lay flat in a large baking dish. Put the pan in the oven while you do step 3.
3. In a large skillet, brown the beef with the sliced onion. Remove from the heat and add the tomato paste mixed with the wine, garlic, oregano, salt, and pepper.
4. Spread the beef mixture over the eggplant slices and set aside while you make the cream sauce.
5. Heat the butter, mix in the flour, and add the milk slowly, stirring with a wire whisk while the sauce thickens. Remove from the heat and add the eggs one at a time. Add salt and Parmesan.
6. Pour the cream sauce over the top of the eggplant-meat layers and bake 1 hour. Let stand 15 minutes before serving.

▪ FRENCH SUMMER SALAD FEST ▪

One-Step Strawberry Soup
French Summer Salad and/or
Avocado with Hearts of Palm and/or
Lentil Salad
Pâté de campagne from the best
    gourmet store
Basket of French bread and assorted rolls
Quick Pots de Crème (page 138) or
    other D. G. dessert

The French are funny. They are purists when it comes to dinner salads, cringing at the thought of a stray slice of tomato mixed in with their greens and classic vinaigrette. But in summer they go hog wild, throwing kitchen sinkfuls of vegetables and cold rice into the salads they eat indoors or take on *pique-nique*.

Kitchen sink salads are fun because if you're creative, they're never the same twice. From the cook's point of view, they are a lovely way to deal with leftovers that would otherwise get tucked into the refrigerator in the name of frugality one week and thrown away moldy in the name of chagrin the next.

Our family is so fond of summer salad suppers, we often build our summer buffets around them. If you vary the colors and textures, you can create a stunning effect with perfectly ordinary ingredients. Add whatever fresh herbs are readily available and you won't recognize the same ingredients you have been eating all winter!

If you don't want an all-salad buffet, add a quiche from Chapter 15 but serve it at room temperature rather than hot. Perk it up with an interesting assortment of breads or muffins.

ONE-STEP STRAWBERRY SOUP

Skip this one if you don't have a food processor.

1	quart strawberries, hulled
2	tablespoons white wine
1	cup (8 ounces) plain yogurt
1	cup (8 ounces) vanilla yogurt

Put all ingredients in the bowl of a food processor with the steel blade in place and process until smooth.

FRENCH SUMMER SALAD

4	cups cooked rice
¼	pound fresh mushrooms, sliced
1	large green pepper, diced
½	small bunch parsley, minced
1	10-ounce package frozen peas, thawed
1	17-ounce can whole kernel corn, drained

1½ cups diced smoked ham
    Tarragon Vinaigrette (page 76)

Mix all the ingredients together in a large, decorative bowl and add Tarragon Vinaigrette to taste. Chill before serving.

AVOCADO WITH HEARTS OF PALM

6 small tomatoes
3 ripe avocados
1 14-ounce can hearts of palm
   Several lettuce leaves
   Tarragon Vinaigrette or Lemon-Dill Dressing (pages 76 and 75 respectively)
6 black and 6 green olives

1. Cut the tomatoes and avocados in quarters and the hearts of palm in 1" pieces.
2. Line a plate with lettuce leaves. Arrange the hearts of palm in the center and surround with alternating quarters of tomato and avocado.
3. Drizzle with the dressing and decorate with the olives.

LENTIL SALAD

½ pound dried lentils
½ pound summer sausage
3 large potatoes, cooked and peeled
2 tomatoes
2 hard-boiled eggs
   Several lettuce leaves
   Tarragon or plain vinaigrette dressing

1. Cover the lentils with water and let them soak overnight. Drain.
2. Slice the summer sausage and potatoes and quarter the tomatoes and hard-boiled eggs.
3. Line a salad bowl with lettuce leaves, place all the other ingredients in the bowl, and toss with the dressing.

▪ HUNGARIAN BUFFET MENU ▪

Kolosvári Káposta
Red Cabbage Slaw
Southern-style biscuits
Hungarian Plum Cake

My mother's sister Annette married the first conductor in the family, a Hungarian-born adopted New Yorker who conducted at the Metropolitan Opera until the School of Music at Indiana University lured him away. The move created a great culinary challenge for my aunt, who was accustomed to entertaining at New York restaurants after the opera. Bloomington, Indiana, didn't have a single restaurant that stayed open after 10 P.M.

Fortunately, she was a creative cook, able to meet the challenge of applauding at the opera house one minute and feeding the hungry at home the next. One of her favorite buffet menus had as its centerpiece a wonderful Hungarian casserole made with pork, rice, and sauerkraut and seasoned with paprika and caraway. It is easy to make and will keep several days in the refrigerator with no loss of flavor.

KÓLOSVÁRI KÁPOSTA

This dish can be prepared as follows or by layering the meat, sauerkraut, and rice and pouring the gravy over the top, ending with additional sour cream. Try it both ways to see which you prefer.

2	onions, sliced
3	to 4 tablespoons vegetable oil
3	pounds cubed pork
3	tablespoons Hungarian paprika
2	teaspoons caraway seeds
1	teaspoon salt
¼	teaspoon pepper
1	6-ounce can tomato paste

    1   cup (8 ounces) sour cream
    2   pounds sauerkraut, drained
    1   cup cooked rice

1. Sauté the onions in the oil in a large casserole. Add the pork, paprika, caraway seeds, salt, and pepper and brown lightly.
2. Add the tomato paste mixed with 2 cups water and cook, covered, until tender.
3. Mix the sour cream into the gravy, then add the sauerkraut and cooked rice.
4. Bake 20 minutes at 400°F. Add more salt, paprika, or sour cream if needed.

RED CABBAGE SLAW

    1   small head red cabbage
    ¼   cup red wine vinegar
    ¼   cup vegetable oil
    2   tablespoons sugar
    1   teaspoon salt
    ¼   teaspoon pepper

Shred the cabbage. Combine the remaining ingredients, pour over the cabbage, and refrigerate, covered, several hours before serving.

HUNGARIAN PLUM CAKE

If small purple Santa Rosa plums happen to be in season, you may want to turn up your air conditioner to get in the mood for this not exactly light fare. You won't be sorry. Hungarian Plum Cake just happens to be the perfect final flourish for these other Magyar delights.

If it's too near the vernal equinox to sight plums, console yourself with an even faster Desperate Gourmet dessert.

    ½   cup (1 stick) butter
    1   cup sugar
    2   eggs
    1   cup flour
    1   teaspoon baking powder
        Pinch salt
    6   ripe purple plums, halved and pitted
    1   teaspoon ground cinnamon

1. Preheat the oven to 375°F.
2. Thoroughly mix the butter with ½ cup of the sugar and the eggs.
3. Mix the flour, baking powder, and salt together and add to the butter mixture.
4. Pour the batter into a greased 8" square baking pan and cover with the plums, skin side down, the other ½ cup sugar, and cinnamon.
5. Bake 30 minutes.

▪ TEX-MEX MERIENDA ▪

Fiesta Dip with Nacho Chips
Taco Salad
Enchiladas with Spinach and Green
   Tomato Sauce
Sun-Dried Anise Cookies

• • • • • • • • • • • • • • • • • •

When we were invited to our first *merienda* shortly after moving to San Antonio in 1986, we had to look up the word. Our Spanish dictionary translated it as "light lunch," but in San Antonio, where Mexican food abounds, a *merienda* can mean a cocktail buffet or late-night supper just as often as a lunch.

Every *merienda* we have attended has been catered and has included live mariachi music played by an authentically costumed band. The food was a colorful spread of Tex-Mex specialties, starting with frozen Margaritas made with a machine that turns ice cubes into snow.

Fortunately, Tex-Mex food is easy enough to prepare yourself, and a little recorded mariachi music is a small investment that will bring the mariachi sound anywhere the real thing is not available.

FIESTA DIP

Fiesta Dip is as delicious as its layers are colorful to behold.

2	9- or 10-ounce cans bean dip or 1 1-pound can refried beans
6	avocados

6	**tablespoons lemon juice**
	Salt and pepper to taste
	Ground cumin to taste
1	**pint sour cream**
½	**pound shredded Cheddar cheese**
½	**pound shredded Monterey Jack cheese**
	Chopped tomatoes and green onions
	Sliced black olives

1. In a large glass bowl, layer the bean dip, then the avocados mashed with the lemon juice and seasonings, then the sour cream, then the cheeses.
2. Top with a mixture of the tomatoes, green onions, and olives.
3. Serve with nacho chips or tostadas and a pie server so guests can scoop through all the layers.

TACO SALAD

For each 4 to 5 servings:

1	**onion**
1	**pound ground beef**
1	**package taco seasoning (I like McCormick best)**
3	**tomatoes**
1	**large head lettuce**
1	**4- to 5-ounce package shredded Cheddar cheese (not imitation)**
1	**11-ounce bag regular size Fritos**

1. Chop the onion coarsely and sauté in a little oil until soft.
2. Add the beef and taco seasoning and cook until the beef is brown, stirring with a fork to break it up.
3. Chop the tomatoes and shred half the lettuce. Mix with the shredded cheese, Fritos, and beef.
4. Line a large salad bowl with the remaining lettuce leaves and fill it with the taco salad mixture. No additional dressing is required.

ENCHILADAS WITH SPINACH AND GREEN TOMATO SAUCE

4	**8½-ounce cans green tomatoes (*tomatitos verdes*), drained**

1	teaspoon minced garlic
1	large onion, in pieces
½	bunch fresh coriander leaves or ½ teaspoon ground coriander
1	teaspoon salt
1	pint sour cream
2	cups peanut oil
12	tortillas
2	10-ounce packages frozen chopped spinach, thawed and squeezed dry
1	pound Monterey Jack cheese, grated

1. In a blender or food processor, put the green tomatoes, garlic, onion, coriander, and salt and process until smooth.
2. Cook 7 minutes in the microwave on high or 30 minutes on the stove. Remove from the heat and stir in the sour cream.
3. Preheat the oven to 325°F.
4. Heat the oil and, when very hot, dip the tortillas first in the oil, then in the sauce.
5. Lay the tortillas flat, put about 1 tablespoon each of the spinach and the grated cheese on top, and roll them up.
6. Place the tortillas side by side in a shallow baking pan, pour the sauce over them, and top with cheese. Bake 20 to 30 minutes.

SUN-DRIED ANISE COOKIES

These cookies take no time to make, look as if an artist sculpted them, have a Mexican flavor, and contain absolutely no fat. In short, a D. G.'s dream of a dessert.

3	eggs
1½	cups sugar
1½	cups flour
1	teaspoon aniseeds

1. In a food processor or with electric mixer, mix all the ingredients until very well blended.
2. Drop by teaspoonfuls onto greased cookie sheets and set out in the sun 2 hours or indoors overnight to dry.
3. Bake 15 minutes at 350°F. Do not brown.

. DINNER FROM MARYLAND'S . EASTERN SHORE

Hot Crab Salad
Avocado Halves with Lemon and Brandy
Fresh Cranberry Relish
Corn Muffins
Intoxicated Mud Pie (page 139) or Self-
**   Frosting Chocolate Cake (page 146)**

Never rent a summer house in an attractive location if you have a lot of friends and want to spend any time out of the kitchen. (If you always take the live-in cook to Southampton for the summer, you don't need this cookbook!) The summer we rented a lovingly re-stored farmhouse on Chesapeake Bay on Maryland's Eastern Shore, I only heard about the wonderful swimming and sailing from our houseguests. Most of my out-of-the-kitchen time was spent pursuing just-caught crab and local produce.

Many dozen cooked-at-the-last-minute hard and soft shell crabs later, I finally got smart. I discovered a crab casserole that actually benefited from being made the day before and reheated. Best of all, despite the variety of ingredients, the crabmeat never loses its identity.

If you don't live where fresh crabmeat is readily available, try making Hot Crab Salad with the new "sea legs" or imitation crab sold in most supermarkets and fish stores these days.

HOT CRAB SALAD

Don't be put off by the number of ingredients in Hot Crab Salad. Once you assemble them, the recipe takes no time to put together.

2	**cups cooked rice**
¼	**cup (½ stick) butter**
¼	**cup lemon juice**
1	**teaspoon dry mustard**

- **1 bunch green onions, chopped**
- **1 pint sour cream**
- **2 cups black olives, halved**
- **3 ounces firm blue cheese**
- **1 pound crabmeat or imitation crabmeat**
- **2 14-ounce cans artichoke hearts, quartered**

1. Preheat the oven to 350°F.
2. Mix the first 4 ingredients in an ovenproof casserole.
3. Mix the next 3 ingredients and add to the first 4.
4. Mix in the remaining ingredients.
5. Bake, covered, 30 minutes.

AVOCADO HALVES WITH LEMON AND BRANDY

- **Juice of 2 large lemons**
- **4 avocados, peeled and halved**
- **1 tablespoon brandy**
- **1 tablespoon mayonnaise**
- **1 teaspoon horseradish sauce**
- **1 tablespoon minced fresh parsley**
- **1 tablespoon minced fresh or 1 teaspoon dried dill**

1. Sprinkle half the lemon juice on the avocados.
2. Mix the remaining ingredients together and spoon 1 teaspoon into each avocado half.
3. Arrange on a platter alone or on lettuce leaves.

FRESH CRANBERRY RELISH

You don't need a recipe for this, but you do need some kind of machine. Just wash and clean a pound of fresh cranberries and chop them up in a food processor or blender with just enough orange juice to moisten the berries and enough sugar to take some of the tartness away. Be sure not to oversugar or the taste won't be refreshing.

Take this tip from the Desperate Gourmet—the less measuring you have to do, the faster you'll get out of the kitchen.

CORN MUFFINS

As for the corn muffins, try to find a supermarket or bakery that makes good ones. There's not much point in spending your limited time making them when you can devote it to the items in this menu that don't come ready-made. If you can't find good corn muffins, make some skillet corn bread. Recipes for it can be found just about anywhere, especially on packages of stone-ground cornmeal.

▪ SUKIYAKI BUFFET MENU ▪

Sukiyaki for Six
White Rice
Undesperate Rum Cake

Our Japanese friends in Hawaii introduced us to Sukiyaki as an interesting, informal way to feed a group of friends. The ingredients are easy to prepare ahead of time and have a real party look when paraded past the guests on platters. The food cooks quickly and sends up inviting aromas in the process. And the end result is so colorful and varied, the only necessary addition to the menu is plain white rice.

If you have a large kitchen and enjoy entertaining your guests in it before dinner, Sukiyaki could turn into your favorite dinner party food. If the kitchen is small or off-limits, you have two other options. Plug in an electric wok or skillet wherever you plan to serve the Sukiyaki and let the guests serve themselves from it. Or transfer the cooked food to a platter and place it on a warming tray for serving.

Since guests really enjoy watching the cooking process, my last choice would be to cook the Sukiyaki in the kitchen while guests consume their cocktails somewhere else.

For some reason, Sukiyaki and rum cake enjoy double billing. Use either the very desperate recipe on page 137 or the one printed here, which takes a little longer but always gets unqualified raves.

SUKIYAKI FOR SIX

The only ingredient in Sukiyaki you may have to look for in an Oriental grocery store is *shirataki*, translucent bean threads that are dry and brittle and come in cellophane packages. They absorb both the liquid and the flavors they are cooked with and add a wonderful texture. While you're shopping, you might want to pick up a bottle of sake (Japanese rice wine) to make the sauce, but dry sherry is a perfectly acceptable substitute.

A word of warning: Sukiyaki is best eaten soon after it is cooked, so don't light the fire at the start of a long cocktail hour.

2	pounds beef tenderloin, sliced paper thin
12	green onions, cut in 2″ lengths
½	head Chinese cabbage, cut in 2″ lengths
½	pound spinach leaves, torn into pieces
1	7- to 8-ounce package *shirataki* (dried bean threads)
12	large mushrooms, sliced
1	8-ounce can sliced bamboo shoots
1	16-ounce package fresh tofu, cut into 1″ cubes
½	cup soy sauce
¼	cup sake or sherry
⅓	cup sugar
2	tablespoons vegetable oil

1. On a large decorative platter, arrange the meat, vegetables, and tofu in groups. Cover and refrigerate until cooking time.
2. Mix the soy sauce, sake, and sugar and set aside.
3. In a large electric skillet or wok, heat the oil and enough sauce to cover the bottom of the pan. Cook the meat about half a minute on one side. Turn and place all the other ingredients and remaining sauce on top.
4. Continue cooking, uncovered, over low heat until the vegetables are just tender. Do not stir.
5. Let the guests serve themselves by spooning white rice into small bowls and spooning the Sukiyaki on top.

UNDESPERATE RUM CAKE

½	cup (1 stick) butter
1¼	cups sugar

2	eggs
2½	cups flour
1	teaspoon baking powder
1	teaspoon baking soda
1	cup plain yogurt
¾	cup raisins

SYRUP
·········

¼	cup dark rum
1	cup water
1	cup sugar
¼	cup orange juice

1. Preheat the oven to 350°F.
2. Cream the butter and sugar and add the eggs one at a time.
3. Sift the flour, baking powder, and soda together and add to the butter-sugar mixture alternately with the yogurt.
4. Stir in the raisins and turn into a greased Bundt pan.
5. Bake 1 hour. While baking, make the syrup.
6. Mix all the syrup ingredients and cook in the microwave 2 minutes or bring to a boil and simmer on top of the stove 5 minutes.
7. Pour the syrup over the warm cake.

■ HOT SOUP AND HORS D'OEUVRES SMORGASBORD ■

D. G. Nabeyaki Udon
Zucchini Soup
Cheese and Pâté Sampler, including Camembert Marinée and Shrimp Pâté (page 78)
Basket of crackers and breads
Smoked Ham with Three D. G. Sauces (page 63)
Finger food desserts (yours or a good bakery's)

• • • • • • • • • • • • • • • • • • •

COLD SOUP AND HORS ▪ D'OEUVRES SMORGASBORD ▪

One-Step Strawberry Soup (page 115)
Cucumber Soup
Cheese and Pâté Sampler, as above
Basket of crackers and breads
Smoked Ham with Three D. G. Sauces
  (page 63)
Finger food desserts, as above

• • • • • • • • • • • • • • • • • • •

The inspiration for the Soup and Hors d'oeuvres Smorgasbord comes from two completely different sources: a restaurant called The Soup Kitchen in Baltimore and a fellowship dinner group called Foyers at St. Mark's Episcopal Church in San Antonio.

At The Soup Kitchen I was introduced to the three-soup sampler lunch. The St. Mark's Foyers group pioneered the all–hors d'oeuvres dinner. For the Desperate Gourmet, the Soup and Hors d'oeuvres Smorgasbord is a creative way out of the cooking and eating doldrums. If you are clever, you can create endless combinations of foods you've made with foods you've bought.

The suggested combinations here include two almost instant soups plus a colorful platter of cheeses designed to contain interesting store-bought varieties plus an easy Camembert marinée you make yourself. The platter of pâtés can boast several of the best you can buy plus a shrimp pâté you and your food processor can mix up in a minute.

If you use decorative leaves or ferns to line your cheese and pâté platters or put crisp parsley in and around all the items, you will end up with a presentation that looks like a work of art and takes almost no time to create. A feat that always reminds me of the pronouncement a famous impresario once made to my husband: "It's not who you are but how you're packaged."

D. G. NABEYAKI UDON

2	3-ounce packages Oriental ramen (noodle soup)
6	dried Chinese mushrooms
¼	to ½ pound boneless chicken breast, sliced
¼	cup *mirin*
1	tablespoon sugar
½	teaspoon soy sauce
1	head Chinese cabbage
	Small bunch green onions, chopped

1. Put the contents of the noodle soup packages in a large pot and add 5 cups boiling water.
2. Add the mushrooms, sliced chicken, and seasonings; cover and let stand ½ to 1 hour.
3. Slice the mushrooms, shred and add the cabbage, and simmer 15 minutes.
4. Add the green onions before serving.

ZUCCHINI SOUP

1	onion
2	pounds zucchini
2	large potatoes
¼	cup (½ stick) butter
2	tablespoons minced fresh dill
1	teaspoon curry powder
1	cup sour cream, sweet cream, or half-and-half (or any combination)

1. Coarsely slice the onion, zucchini, and potato.
2. Melt the butter in a large skillet and add the vegetables, dill, curry powder, and 1 quart water. Cook 15 minutes.
3. Puree the soup in a food processor or blender and add the cream just before serving. Reheat very gently if not serving immediately so the cream doesn't curdle.

CAMEMBERT MARINÉE

1	whole ripe Camembert
	Dry white wine

½ cup (1 stick) butter
    Finely chopped almonds

1. Soak the cheese in wine to cover overnight.
2. Drain and scrape the cheese, but leave some of the crust.
3. Mix the cheese with the softened butter and chill until firm. Cover with almonds before serving.

CUCUMBER SOUP

3   cucumbers, peeled and seeded
2   teaspoons minced garlic
1   green pepper
1   teaspoon dried oregano
1   cup sour cream
1½ cups plain yogurt
2   tablespoons minced fresh dill
    Salt and pepper to taste

1. Put all but the dill, salt, and pepper in the food processor and process until smooth.
2. Add the dill, salt, and pepper. Serve very cold.

OLD-FASHIONED
■ BACKYARD BARBECUE ■

Fifties Cheese Canapés
Barbecued Whole Brisket
Bourbon Baked Beans
Garden Potato Salad
Iced tea and homemade lemonade
Tim's "Best of Show" Cheesecake (page 148)

Even if you don't have kids, an outdoor meal of barbecued brisket, home-baked beans, and old-fashioned potato salad is a refreshing change from "uptown food." It's honest, unsubtle and just plain good for the soul. Myth or no, it reminds us of simpler days when people were content with where they were, particularly from the vantage point of their own backyard on a summer Sunday afternoon. Serve the grown-ups hot bubbly cheese canapés from the fifties, and they'll be in heaven.

FIFTIES CHEESE CANAPÉS

If you're old enough to remember what you ate in the fifties, you will probably appreciate the nostalgia trip of hot, bubbly Cheese Canapés. They are simple and delicious in a completely non-look-how-chic-and-clever-I-am way. The only change I have made to bring them up to date is to repeal the instructions to cut the bread into rounds and substitute easier-to-cut squares. This recipe makes 24 canapés.

½   cup mayonnaise
¼   cup freshly grated Parmesan cheese
1   teaspoon garlic powder
1   teaspoon dried oregano
6   slices thin white bread, crusts removed

1. Preheat the oven to 400°F.
2. Mix the first 4 ingredients together and spread evenly on the bread.
3. Bake on an ungreased cookie sheet 10 to 15 minutes or until the cheese is bubbly and the top slightly brown.
4. Cut each canapé in quarters and serve hot.

BARBECUED WHOLE BRISKET

1   whole beef brisket (8 to 10 pounds)
    Salt and pepper
2   cups ketchup
1   tablespoon Pickapeppa or Worcestershire sauce
1   tablespoon vegetable oil
1   teaspoon liquid smoke
1   teaspoon seasoned salt

1. Rub the meat with salt and pepper, wrap in foil, and cook slowly over charcoal 4 to 6 hours or until done the way you like it.
2. Cook the remaining ingredients in the microwave oven until well blended or bring to a boil on top of the stove and simmer 5 minutes.
3. Pass the sauce with the cooked brisket.

BOURBON BAKED BEANS

3	1-pound cans baked beans
¼	cup bourbon
½	cup strong black coffee
1	8-ounce can sliced pineapple

1. Four hours before serving, mix the beans, bourbon, and coffee in an oven-to-table serving dish and let stand, covered, at room temperature.
2. One hour before serving, remove the cover and bake 45 minutes at 375°F.
3. Decorate the sides of the casserole with slices of pineapple cut in half and bake 15 minutes longer.

GARDEN POTATO SALAD

Since everyone assumes that no self-respecting Desperate Gourmet would ever dream of making potato salad, prepare your response to the inevitable "*Where* did you get this potato salad? It's fantastic."

12	medium potatoes
1	onion, sliced
2	tablespoons seasoned salt
1	teaspoon celery seeds
¼	cup vegetable oil
¼	cup yellow mustard
1	cup mayonnaise
¼	cup pickle relish

1. Cook the potatoes in water until barely done, then peel and cut them into bite-size pieces.
2. Mix all the other ingredients, toss with the potatoes, and chill.

THE DESPERATE GOURMET'S INDOOR PICNIC

Welcome to "Who Invited All These Tacky People, Part II," which is doomsday compared to Part I because none of the old D. G. secrets and shortcuts will bail you out this time.

This time the dinner party you planned is just around the corner when emergency strikes. A "do it yesterday" deadline at work, a sick relative at home or on the other side of town, a drop-in guest or a personal crisis of gargantuan proportions. The reason doesn't matter. The reality is your dinner party has been pushed to last place on the priority list and there isn't a thing you can do about it.

You don't want to cancel; you can't or won't move the festivities to the nearest restaurant; it's too late to hire a caterer; and you don't want catering by carry-out. You're stuck, right?

Wrong! With a little assembly of simple props during one of your undesperate moments, you can stage The Desperate Gourmet's Indoor Picnic and amuse your guests while feeding them with practically no work.

First, the props:

- As many attractive meal-size baskets as you intend to have guests. (A store like Pier 1 is a good source for baskets.)
- An equal number of gaily colored cloth dinner napkins, either solid or patterned, depending on whether your baskets are plain or multi-colored. Choose a dacron-cotton blend that won't need ironing the next time they're washed and worn.
- Good-quality (that means heavy) plastic forks and spoons. Check around. Most well-stocked party stores carry these in gorgeous colors. A far cry from the flimsy white ones that used to be "it" for plastic.

- Equally good-quality matching paper or plastic plates.
- Paper napkins in a matching exotic color or with some unusual design. It's worth the trouble of tracking down a good store that sells artistic paper party products because, once found, you can make a beeline to it whenever desperation strikes again.
- A small party favor you can tuck into each basket as a consolation prize for the corners you have had to cut. Let your mind wander back to the best stocking stuffers from last Christmas and you'll come up with something. If you are looking to amuse, try the printed Post-it notes or a package of cocktail napkins with a saying like "Love Your Enemies. It Drives Them Crazy."
- As many silk or other good-quality artificial flowers as there are baskets (buy them in two different colors if you are going to have different favors for men and women).
- 5- or 8-ounce size disposable plastic cups, either clear or decorated, or small plastic cups with snap-on lids if you can find them.

That's it for the props. Buy and stash them for emergency use only and you're all set.

When emergency strikes, buy the food and assemble the baskets.

The food:

- You guessed it, fried chicken. Be sure to pick the best available source. Some places will cook it to order with special spices or make it crustier (and less greasy!) than usual just for you. Order two large pieces or three smaller ones per person.
- Salads. If you're using a fast food chain for the chicken, don't buy their potato salad, cole slaw,

or dinner rolls. Choose gourmet salads from the highest-quality take-out shop in your area and try to find something with a lot more pizzazz than the standard fried chicken companions. Use pasta salads, fresh fruit salads, artichoke-hearts-and-anything salads.

- Rolls. Use breads, rolls, croissants, or muffins from the best bakery in town. Butter the rolls if they're plain.
- Dessert. The best-quality cookies (something different would be lovely if you can find it) or brownies available. Definitely finger food.

Just before the guests arrive, put it all together:

- Line each basket with a cloth napkin.
- Wire an artificial flower onto each basket so that it is sticking straight up. Use one color for men, another for women if your favors are differentiated.
- Tuck a plate, plastic fork, and paper napkin into the corner of each basket and put the chicken on the opposite side.
- Pack the salads into the small plastic containers with snap-on lids or into the plastic cups with plastic wrap over the top and put them in the basket.
- Place the buttered rolls, bread, or muffins in the baskets.
- Wrap the cookies in plastic or use small plastic bags and put them in the baskets.
- Put the favors (wrap them if they didn't come in plastic) on top and pull the corners of the cloth napkins down around the contents of the baskets.

Last but not least:

- Put your prettiest cloth on the dining table (or on whatever surface you will serve from) and line up the filled baskets.

- Prepare your well-stocked bar for service, put on a record, tape, or disk (the music from *Picnic* would be a nice if subtle touch, or the music from Sondheim's latest, *Into the Woods*).

And, finally:

When the doorbell rings, relax and enjoy the fun. After what you've been through this week, you've earned it!

· 19 ·

D.G. DESSERTS, OR DON'T CREAM THE BUTTER AND SUGAR

IF you're really a Desperate Gourmet, any dessert recipe that begins with instructions to "cream the butter and sugar" is a mandate to turn the page in search of something else. "Cream the butter and sugar" invariably leads to other time-consuming commands like "sift the flour and baking powder." Definitely not music to the D. G.'s ears.

Not that I wouldn't love to spend a leisurely Saturday morning making old-fashioned apple strudel. I just can't seem to remember the last Saturday morning I could spare for the preparation of a single item on a menu.

When you're desperate, you're desperate, and the gourmet five-minute dessert is definitely in order. For your desperation pleasure, I submit twenty desserts in two categories. The first consists entirely of no-cook entries. They are elegant enough to finish off the most formal dinner party but simple enough to turn out at the drop of a "What's for dessert?"

All ten recipes in the second category can be created without the benefit of a single machine—mixer, blender, food processor—or even a sifter! The only equipment you need to play this game is a bowl and a wooden spoon, and you'll win by a mile.

NO-COOK DESSERTS

Rum Cake and Strawberries in Champagne win the no-work prize in the dessert category. Their strong suits are good basic ingredients and effortless simplicity. They are no more trouble than a trip to the local bakery or fruit stand and still qualify as homemade and unusual.

RUM CAKE

If you have trouble finding sponge cakes in your city in the winter, try something else while waiting for the spring thaw.

For four portions:

> 3 **tablespoons brandy**
> 4 **individual sponge cakes (store-bought, of course)**
> **Blackberry or guava jelly**
> ⅓ **cup dark rum**

1. Pour the brandy into the center of each sponge cake and then fill with jelly.
2. Pour the rum over the outside of the cakes and serve. Not enough fanfare? Ignite before serving.

STRAWBERRIES IN CHAMPAGNE

This dessert should be served in glass dessert dishes or wineglasses to show it off to best advantage. To win high honors, all you need is whole strawberries (preferably fresh, but frozen without sugar will do), sugar, and champagne better than the $2.98 variety but nowhere near $40 a bottle.

For a change, use sliced fresh peaches when they're in season.

> **2** quarts strawberries, washed and hulled, with or
> without stems
> Sugar
> Champagne

1. Sprinkle the strawberries with sugar and chill in 8 individual glass
   dishes.
2. Just before serving, fill the dishes of strawberries with champagne.
3. Serve with butter cookies or other plain cookies on the side.

QUICK POTS DE CRÈME

Like chocolate mousse, this is one of the great French desserts. The reason
I prefer pots de crème to chocolate mousse is that it tastes just as rich
but doesn't use whipped cream. The D. G. version is as good as the
original but it takes no longer to produce than, perish the thought, instant
chocolate pudding.

> **½** cup whole milk
> **1** 12-ounce package semisweet chocolate chips (not
>   imitiation chocolate)
> **2** eggs
> **¼** cup sugar
> **1** tablespoon dark rum (or 1 teaspoon vanilla
>   extract, if you prefer)

1. Heat the milk to boiling. (Do this in the microwave if you have one.)
2. Put all the other ingredients in a blender or food processor, add the
   milk and process about 1 minute.
3. Pour into 8 small dessert dishes and chill.

AMARETTO SOUFFLÉ

The original recipe for this soufflé calls for heavy cream and egg yolks.
How close this far less time-consuming and lower calorie/cholesterol version comes to the original depends largely on the quality of the ice cream
you use. Choose one with the least additives and the most flavor.

> **1** quart top-quality vanilla ice cream
> **⅓** cup amaretto liqueur
> **1** cup finely crushed almond macaroons

1. Soften the ice cream and combine it with the amaretto and all but 2 tablespoons of the macaroon crumbs.
2. Spoon the mixture into a soufflé dish and sprinkle the reserved crumbs on top. Freeze until ready to serve.

FRESH ORANGE ICE

After a heavy winter dinner or on a hot summer evening, Fresh Orange Ice is one of the most refreshing desserts you can serve. Everyone will be very impressed that you made it "from scratch." What they won't know, unless you tell them, is that the preparation time is under 5 minutes!

> **1 cup water**
> **1 cup sugar**
> **Juice of 2 oranges**
> **1 egg white, stiffly beaten**

1. Boil the water and sugar about 2 minutes on top of the stove or in the microwave.
2. Combine the sugar water with the orange juice and freeze in a metal ice cube tray, bowl, or loaf pan.
3. When frozen (it won't get solid), fold in the stiffly beaten egg white and return to the freezer in individual dessert dishes.

INTOXICATED MUD PIE

Intoxicated Mud Pie is one of the great D. G. standbys. I have yet to find anyone who doesn't love it, and its D. G. qualities are just as sterling. Two are just as easy to make as one and the second will live happily in the freezer for months. With mud pie in the freezer, I know I'm safe to issue a spontaneous invitation for dessert and coffee anytime. If spontaneous invitations are not your style, it can't be all bad to have the dessert already prepared when your next dinner party is only in the planning stage.

> **1 quart coffee or other suitable flavor ice cream**
> **3 tablespoons brandy (or more, to taste)**
> **1 chocolate cookie crumb pie shell**
> **1 jar real fudge sauce (the best you can find)**

1. Let the ice cream soften enough to mix in the brandy.
2. Pile the ice cream into the pie shell and freeze until hard.
3. Spread the fudge sauce over the top and return to the freezer until ready to serve.

ALL SEASON SUMMER PUDDING

This is the Desperate Gourmet version of a traditional English summer pudding made with fresh berries. Aside from the obvious seasonal advantage, the D. G. version also eliminates the need to cook the fruit. The recipe couldn't be simpler and can be made in whatever shape you prefer, from a round bowl to a loaf pan. When the berries soak through the bread, the pudding turns a beautiful strawberry color.

8	**slices (approximately) white bread**
2	**10-ounce boxes frozen strawberries with sugar, thawed**

1. Trim the crusts off the bread and line the bottom and sides of a greased bowl or loaf pan with them. Be sure the slices touch on all sides.
2. Puree the fruit in a blender or food processor (or mash it by hand) and pour it over the bread.
3. Cover the top with bread slices, place a bowl or dish on top to weight it down, and refrigerate overnight. Unmold to serve.

BRANDY ALEXANDER PIE

When I first started making Brandy Alexander Pie, I thought nothing of decorating the top with additional whipped cream. I still make this pie (my theory being that less than an ounce of cream never killed anyone not on a restricted diet), but now I decorate the top with fruit in the shape of a flower. There are plenty of other decorative possibilities, which I leave to your imagination and the resources of your pantry.

1	**envelope unflavored gelatin**
½	**cup cold water**
⅔	**cup sugar**
¼	**teaspoon salt**
3	**eggs, separated**
¼	**cup cognac**
¼	**cup Kahlua or crème de cacao**
1	**cup heavy cream, whipped**
1	**graham cracker pie shell**

1. Sprinkle the gelatin over the cold water, add ⅓ cup of the sugar, the salt and egg yolks, and heat to dissolve and thicken.
2. Stir in the cognac and Kahlua and chill about 15 minutes.
3. Beat the egg whites until stiff, then beat in the remaining sugar and fold into the gelatin mixture.
4. Fold in the whipped cream and turn into the crust. Chill. Serve plain or decorate the top before serving.

MACÉDOINE OF GRAPES

Macédoine de Fruits often appears as a dessert item on the menus of fine restaurants. Literally a medley of fruits, it is instantly an elegant light dessert of fresh fruits and a splash of light spirits. Now that seedless grapes come in colors other than green, you can make a lovely macédoine by mixing red and green grapes, equal splashes of sweet and dry vermouth, and a hint of cinnamon. Best of all, it doesn't take much longer than opening one of those infernal cans of fruit cocktail.

>   ½   pound each green and red seedless grapes
>   ¼   cup each sweet and dry vermouth
>   Sugar to taste (up to ¼ cup)
>   2   pinches ground cinnamon

1. Divide the grapes among 4 or 5 dessert dishes.
2. Mix all the other ingredients, pour over the grapes, and chill.

MOCHA PARFAITS

These parfaits can be made with or without rum. The best D. G. feature is that the whole tastes as if it is far greater than the sum of its parts. Translation: you get credit for being the author of a sumptuous creation far simpler than your guests will ever dream.

>   3   tablespoons instant coffee
>   3   tablespoons dark brown sugar
>   2   tablespoons boiling water
>   2   quarts French vanilla ice cream
>   ½   cup dark rum (optional)

1. Mix the coffee and sugar together and add the boiling water.
2. Mix the ice cream with the rum and coffee mixture.
3. Spoon into parfait dishes or wineglasses and freeze overnight.

MAGIC WITHOUT MACHINES

When it comes to desserts, I feel like the woman who always asked, "How many pots?" whenever she was offered a new recipe. If it took more than one or two, she would have none of it. While no one can survive without entrees, making desserts is a luxury. Especially when you've used the food processor for the main course and would much rather throw it in the dishwasher than wash it by hand and crank it up again to make dessert.

For a Desperate Gourmet, the best desserts are those that can be made in one or two simple operations with no loss of quality. After years of stalking, I submit the following prey, all of which can be created in minutes without the aid of a single twentieth-century machine!

ALMOST INSTANT PECAN PIE

The acid test of the Almost Instant Pecan Pie I have made for years was serving it to some of the country's real pecan aficionados just after we moved to San Antonio, one of the great pecan capitals. When several people said it was better than their grandmothers', I knew I had a real treasure to share.

3	eggs, lightly beaten
1	cup dark corn syrup
1	cup sugar
2	tablespoons butter or margarine, melted
1	teaspoon vanilla extract
1½	cups broken pecans
1	9″ frozen pie shell, slightly thawed

1. Preheat the oven to 350°F.
2. Put all the ingredients except the pecans in a bowl and stir with a wooden spoon until just mixed.
3. Stir in the pecans, pour into the pie shell, and bake 1 hour.

MINI MANSIONS' LEMON CHESS PIE

Mini Mansions is a unique and wonderful combination tea room, religious bookstore, and gift shop in San Antonio. I begged for the recipe for their Lemon Chess Pie, which is the best I have ever tasted. When they graciously shared it, I was delighted. But when I tried it, I was doubly pleased to find that it had all the D. G. characteristics without an iota of adaptation. I highly recommend lunch at the Mini Mansions tearoom to anyone within traveling distance of San Antonio. If not, be sure to make the Lemon Chess Pie yourself.

2	cups sugar
1	tablespoon flour
1	tablespoon cornmeal
4	eggs
¼	cup milk
¼	cup fresh lemon juice
¼	cup (½ stick) butter, melted
1	tablespoon freshly grated lemon rind
1	9″ unbaked pie shell

1. Preheat the oven to 350°F.
2. With a wire whisk, mix the first 4 ingredients.
3. Add the next 4 ingredients, one at a time.
4. Pour into the pie shell and bake about 1 hour or until set. (The top should be golden, not brown.)

ATHENIAN WALNUT CAKE

If you love the taste of baklava but have no interest in fooling around with phyllo dough, which is as temperamental as it is time-consuming, you will love the following recipe for Athenian Walnut Cake. I know it is authentic because it was called *karithopita* when I acquired it from a friend's Greek mother-in-law. It has the wonderful honey-nut taste of baklava but entails none of the hard work.

½	cup (1 stick) sweet butter at room temperature
1	cup sugar
3	eggs, slightly beaten
2	teaspoons baking powder

> 1   **teaspoon ground cinnamon**
>   **Pinch salt**
> 2   **cups flour**
> 2   **cups chopped walnuts**

SYRUP
· · · · · · · · ·

> 2   **cups honey**
> 1   **cup water**

1. Preheat the oven to 350°F.
2. Beat the butter and sugar with a wooden spoon. Add the eggs.
3. Stir the baking powder, cinnamon, salt, and flour together and mix in the butter mixture until soft and pliable.
4. Add the walnuts and bake in a greased loaf pan 30 to 35 minutes or until the top is golden brown.
5. To make the syrup, boil the honey and water 5 minutes and pour over the warm cake. Let stand 1 hour before serving.

BANANAS FLAMBÉ
· ·

The funny thing about Bananas Flambé is that everyone is always surprised and delighted when they appear for dessert, yet people rarely serve them. That suits the Desperate Gourmet just fine, since the recipe would lose a lot of its appeal if it were the sort that guests would take one look at and think "Oh, that." Bananas Flambé can be made very simply with brown sugar, butter, and rum, but I think the addition of a little fresh lime juice and a few spices transforms it to a loftier realm.

> 6   **ripe bananas**
>   **Juice of 1 lime**
> ½   **teaspoon each ground cinnamon, cloves, and**
>   **nutmeg**
> ½   **cup brown sugar**
> ¼   **cup (½ stick) butter**
> ½   **cup light or dark rum**

1. Peel and slice bananas and place them in a baking dish.
2. Sprinkle with lime juice, spices, and sugar and dot with butter.
3. Bake 10 minutes at 375°F or 3 minutes in the microwave.
4. Add rum, and ignite *carefully*.

CONGO COOKIES

When Harborplace, the Rouse Company's glass pavilioned shopping mall, opened in Baltimore's Inner Harbor, one of the most popular food stalls offered a sinfully rich cookie creation whose name I have forgotten. I'm sure they would never divulge their recipe, but by a lucky coincidence I have had the same recipe for years under the name Congo Cookies. They are so good I would probably put my schedule out to pasture just to make them. Fortunately, they are one of the fastest cookies to make and you don't have to drop, roll, mold, or shape them! This recipe makes extra to freeze.

1	cup vegetable oil
1	1-pound box dark brown sugar
3	eggs
1	teaspoon almond extract
2½	cups flour
2½	teaspoons baking powder
1	teaspoon salt
1	12-ounce package semisweet chocolate chips
1	cup chopped pecans (optional)

1. Preheat the oven to 350°F.
2. Mix the oil, sugar, eggs, and almond extract.
3. Mix the dry ingredients with your fingers or a wooden spoon and add the chocolate chips, nuts, and sugar mixture.
4. Turn into a pan 9½″ × 15″ × 2″ and bake 30 to 35 minutes. Cut into small squares because they are very rich.

PINEAPPLE CARROT CAKE

I thought I had come up with the perfect D. G. recipe for carrot cake—one that uses baby food carrots and gets mixed with a wooden spoon—until we moved to Hawaii. There I discovered that adding crushed pineapple creates a little miracle of moistness, texture, and flavor. Try it for breakfast as well as dessert.

3	cups flour
1	teaspoon baking soda
1	teaspoon baking powder

> 1 **teaspoon ground cinnamon**
> 2 **cups sugar**
> ⅛ **cup vegetable oil**
> 3 **eggs**
> 2 **4½-ounce jars strained carrots (baby food)**
> 1 **8-ounce can crushed pineapple in juice**
> 2 **teaspoons vanilla extract**
> 1 **cup sliced almonds**

1. Preheat the oven to 350°F.
2. Mix the first 4 ingredients with your fingers and set aside.
3. Beat the sugar, oil, and eggs with a wooden spoon and add the carrots, the pineapple with its juice, and the vanilla and nuts.
4. Mix in the dry ingredients and bake in a greased tube or Bundt pan 1 hour and 15 minutes.

SELF-FROSTING CHOCOLATE CAKE

What could be more appealing to a Desperate Gourmet than a rich chocolate cake that makes its own frosting as it bakes? Believe it or not, this little wonder can be stirred up in a single bowl with no blending, beating, or anything more energetic than light mixing. Make this often and you'll be the best friend of every chocoholic in the neighborhood.

> 1 **cup sifted flour**
> 2 **teaspoons baking powder**
> ¼ **teaspoon salt**
> 1¼ **cups sugar**
> 6½ **tablespoons unsweetened cocoa**
> ¾ **cup milk**
> 2 **tablespoons butter, melted**
> 1 **teaspoon vanilla extract**
> ½ **cup brown sugar**
> 1 **cup water**

1. Preheat the oven to 350°F.
2. Mix the flour, baking powder, salt, ¾ cup of the sugar, and 1½ tablespoons of the cocoa in a bowl, then stir in the milk, butter, and vanilla.
3. Spread evenly in a greased cake pan.
4. In the microwave or on top of the stove, heat the remaining white sugar, cocoa, brown sugar, and water until melted and pour over the batter.
5. Bake 40 minutes, cool, and turn bottom up.

PEACH KUCHEN

This is one of the most heavenly desserts I know. It is best made with fresh peaches, but when they are not in season, you can use frozen peach halves or slices instead. Don't be horrified by the cream and the egg yolks. Each serving doesn't end up with very much of either, and the result is so special it's worth cutting down somewhere else or pumping a little more iron to erase the damage. If this sounds too flip for these enlightened times, it isn't. I can advertise with pride that after twenty years of using the recipes in this book, both my husband's and my cholesterol counts are enviably low, which can't be all heredity.

2	cups flour
¼	teaspoon baking powder
½	teaspoon salt
1	cup sugar
½	cup (1 stick) soft butter
6	peaches, sliced, or 2 packages frozen sliced peaches
2	teaspoons ground cinnamon
2	egg yolks
1	cup heavy cream

1. Preheat the oven to 400°F.
2. Mix the flour, baking powder, salt, and 2 tablespoons of the sugar together, then work in the butter with your fingers until it has the texture of coarse cornmeal. Pat into an 8" square pan.
3. Arrange the peach slices on top and sprinkle with cinnamon and remaining sugar.
4. Bake 15 minutes. Mix the egg yolks with the cream and pour on top. Bake 35 minutes longer.

DATE CAKE CASABLANCA

The unusual feature of moist, dark Date Cake Casablanca is its coffee content. Use instant only if you never brew the real thing. Despite what the ads say, you *can* taste the difference.

¾	cup hot coffee
¾	cup boiling water
1	pound pitted dates
1	teaspoon baking soda

> 1½ cups sugar
> 2   eggs
> 1   tablespoon butter
> 1⅓ cups flour
> 1   cup chopped nuts
>   Pinch salt

1. Preheat the oven to 325°F.
2. Pour the coffee and water on the dates and baking soda and let stand 5 minutes.
3. Mix all the other ingredients, add the date mixture, and bake in a greased 8″ square pan 45 minutes.

TIM'S "BEST OF SHOW" CHEESECAKE

Our son Timothy would forsake all other desserts for good cheesecake. He orders it whenever he finds it on a restaurant menu and over the years has probably tried out more versions than anyone would want to count. A self-proclaimed noncook, his one culinary claim to fame (surprise, surprise!) is cheesecake, which he learned to make because no one (namely me) could stand to make it as often as he wanted to eat it. He really scoured the countryside for the best available recipe and must have sampled at least twenty-five in the process. If you like cheesecake, I think you will find the final choice "Best of Show."

If you have a microwave, you can mix up the whole thing in about 2 minutes. Without one, you may have to put the cream cheese in the oven to soften it if, like me, you'll do almost anything to avoid getting out the old mixer.

> 1   pound best-quality cream cheese, softened
>   Juice of 2 lemons (3 if small)
> 1   cup sugar
> ¼   cup flour
> 2   eggs
> 1   graham cracker pie shell

1. Mix all the ingredients until smooth and pour into the pie shell.
2. Bake 1 hour at 250°F, turn off the oven, and leave it in the oven all day or overnight. *Or* bake it 50 minutes to 1 hour at 350°F. *Or*, best of all, which we discovered by accident, prepare the pie and re-

frigerate it, covered and *unbaked*, for 2 days and then bake it 50 minutes to 1 hour at 350°F. The texture is out of this world. The only hard part for a Desperate Gourmet is knowing what you're going to have for dessert 2 days in advance!

3. Whichever baking method you choose, serve the cheesecake chilled.

· 20 ·

THE DESPERATE GOURMET DOES CHRISTMAS

REMEMBER the Super Mom era when women were not only expected to be all things to all people, they even had to pretend they were succeeding? Those were the Bad Old Days when everyone in general and Madison Avenue in particular conspired to convince us that everyone *else* was working full-time and still baking merrily, decorating creatively, dressing smashingly, and mothering patiently, so why were you the only shrew who was feeling overwhelmed, screaming at the kids, and had no presents under the tree on December 23?

Fortunately, Super Mom is dead and it is now not only okay but fashionable to be "stressed out." Christmas cookies that look home-made can now be purchased without guilt, and even the curmudgeon on your Christmas list can be appeased without any more effort than phoning in the order for his gift from the catalog in which you've picked it out.

The best news about this decrease in accountability and in-crease in availability is that it frees us to do something special at

Christmas for the people who make our life worth living the rest of the year. Here are a few Desperate Gourmet ideas that say "You are special" to selected people on your Christmas list.

The Desperate Gourmet "Come for Cocktails" Gift Basket

This is an appropriate gift for all ages, from grown children in their first apartment to the grandmother who only entertains occasionally to all your friends who are just as desperate as you are and never seem to have anything to nibble on when you stop by for a drink.

Check out the suggested pop-top hors d'oeuvres in Chapter 14 and pick four to six for each basket you intend to make. Pick out a package of unusually funny or unusually pretty cocktail napkins for each basket, then buy the baskets themselves and some pretty fabric or tissue to line them. Write a message like "Merry Christmas from one Desperate Gourmet to another" on the gift tags and rejoice in the knowledge that your gift may save someone's life for up to six months.

If you want a more lavish variation on this theme, tuck a bottle or two of spirits into the basket, or the fixings for a Desperate Gourmet special like Danish Mary à la Alfred (page 86) and the recipe to go with it.

Homemade Boursin from the Desperate Gourmet

Make a recipe of Homemade Boursin (page 78) and fill a set of four individual soufflé dishes for each person to whom you intend to give this gift. Cover the dishes carefully with plastic wrap and freeze until ready to give, either in a decorated basket or a mini shopping bag lined with colored tissue. Copy the recipe onto a card and tuck it in with each gift so the recipient will be able to make it in the future. If you prefer, you can tuck the recipe in the empty soufflé dishes and let the recipient whip up this almost instant hors d'oeuvre.

A Desperate Gourmet Quiche in a Fluted Ceramic Quiche Dish

Make one of the quiche recipes on pages 71–73, and freeze it until gift time. Pop it into a ceramic quiche dish for a lovely gift. *Or* write out the recipes for all three Desperate Gourmet quiches in this book and give them along with the quiche dish.

Glazed Pecans in a Christmas Tin or Pretty Candy Dish

This is one of the easiest and most delicious things you can do with shelled pecan halves.

GLAZED PECANS

3 cups pecan halves
½ cup sugar
¼ cup water
2 teaspoons unsweetened cocoa or instant coffee
½ teaspoon ground cinnamon
Pinch salt

Boil all the ingredients 3 to 5 minutes. Spread on wax paper to cool. Pack in decorated Christmas tins or put in glass or ceramic candy dishes.

RASPBERRY MERINGUE KISSES

What is Christmas without at least one homemade cookie? This one turns out a beautiful shade of deep pink, mounds itself into a pretty shape, and is easy enough for kids to make for their friends.

4 egg whites
⅔ cup sugar
1 small box raspberry gelatin
1 teaspoon vanilla extract
1 12-ounce package semisweet chocolate chips

1. Preheat the oven to 375°F.
2. Beat the egg whites until stiff, then stir in the remaining ingredients.
3. Drop by teaspoonfuls on ungreased cookie sheets, put in the oven, and count to 10. Turn off the oven and leave overnight.

RUM-BOURBON BALLS

My husband would forgo all other Christmas desserts for Rum-Bourbon Balls. They are sinfully rich, don't need to be cooked or baked, but they do have to be rolled into small balls. If you can find a child to do this for you, you've got it made with just about every adult on your gift list. Pile them in small decorated tins for gifts.

2	cups cinnamon crisp cookie crumbs
¼	cup unsweetened cocoa (I prefer Droste's)
1	teaspoon ground cinnamon
1	teaspoon grated orange rind
⅓	cup dark rum
	Bourbon just to moisten
1	cup confectioner's sugar

1. Mix all the ingredients but the bourbon and confectioner's sugar. Moisten with just enough bourbon to make the mixture hold together.
2. Form into small balls and roll in the confectioner's sugar.

The Very Best Fruitcake with No "Red and Green Things"

I grew up thinking I hated fruitcake because I couldn't stand those hard, funny-tasting red and green things in it. By the time I learned they were artificially colored candied citron, I had finally tasted a heavenly fruitcake that didn't come with any. Many Christmases later I am convinced this is the best fruitcake there is. The recipe is not exactly desperate, but it's easier than most, and whoever receives it will thank you all year.

THE VERY BEST FRUITCAKE

3	cups presifted flour
1	pound golden raisins
1	pound broken pecans
1	teaspoon salt
1	teaspoon baking soda
1	tablespoon warm water
1	pound soft butter
2	cups sugar

| 6 | eggs, separated |
| ¼ | cup Grand Marnier liqueur |

1. Preheat the oven to 250°F.
2. Mix the first 4 ingredients with your hands. Dissolve the baking soda in the water.
3. In a blender or food processor, combine the dissolved baking soda with the butter, sugar, egg yolks, and Grand Marnier. Add to the flour mixture.
4. Beat the egg whites until stiff and fold into the batter.
5. Bake in a greased Bundt pan 2½ hours.

Christmas Ham with One, Two, or Three Desperate Gourmet Sauces

Check page 63 for the three fabulous sauces you can make in seconds. Pour them into pretty glass jars with hand-lettered labels on them.

Specialty Items from the Desperate Gourmet's Basic Pantry and the Recipes to Go with Them

Take a trip to the nearest Oriental, Greek, or Middle Eastern grocery store and stock up on Desperate Gourmet items for yourself and a few gifts. Be sure to wrap up recipes along with your special groceries.

A "Great Dinners for Eight" Menu, the Recipes, and All the Items on the Shopping List to Go with It

For Someone Extra Special: The Whole Desperate Gourmet Basic Bar or Pantry

· 21 ·

DARK SECRETS OF THE DESPERATE GOURMET

· · · · · · · · · · · · · · · · · · ·

HERE are a few final tips and shortcuts devised by this Desperate Gourmet for the millions of kindred spirits I know are out there.

TAKE CONTROL OF YOUR KITCHEN. Instead of standing around waiting for something to simmer, bake, or boil, make something happen. Squeeze a few lemons and whip up some Lemon-Dill Dressing or make balls out of ice cream and roll them in nuts so you always have a special dessert.

STAY ON THE LOOKOUT FOR POP-TOP HORS D'OEUVRES. As soon as you find something exotic that comes in a package, grab a bunch and serve it until everyone else finds it too.

NEVER MAKE ONLY ONE QUICHE. Even if you're the Mother Hubbard of the freezer, try to keep one of these versatile little treasures inside at all times.

IF YOU'RE A DESPERATE GOURMET, "NOTHING" IS THE WRONG ANSWER TO ANY GUEST'S "WHAT CAN I BRING?" Desperation is well known to those who ask, and the offer is invariably sincere.

SINCE A WELL-STOCKED PANTRY IS THE DESPERATE GOURMET'S SECRET WEAPON, grit your teeth and install a pad and pencil on the inside of one of your kitchen cabinet doors.

KEEP A CLOSED JAR OF FETA CHEESE AND A FEW GREEK OLIVES IN YOUR REFRIGERATOR AND YOU'LL ALWAYS BE ABLE TO WHIP UP A GREEK SALAD when ordinary salads are boring you to tears.

CHECK THE SHARPNESS OF YOUR KITCHEN KNIVES OFTEN. Dull knives waste time that no Desperate Gourmet can afford to give away.

WHEN ENTERTAINING, REMEMBER TO START THE COFFEE AND FILL THE SUGAR AND CREAMER BEFORE YOUR GUESTS ARRIVE.

TRY TO STAKE OUT A SPECIAL DRAWER OR CABINET FOR ALL YOUR NAPKINS, CANDLES, PLACE CARDS, AND OTHER PARTY PARAPHERNALIA so you can make a beeline for supplies on less than a moment's notice.

IN CASE OF EMERGENCY—the roast gets ruined, the potatoes burn, you stayed at the office too late to go to the grocery store—keep a small collection of menus from restaurants that deliver.

EVEN IF YOU HAVE NO MORE GROWING SPACE THAN A WINDOWSILL, TRY TO FILL IT WITH ONE OR TWO FRESH HERBS. A handful of fresh basil or marjoram will put gourmet flavor into even the simplest foods.

MEMORIZE THE MENUS FOR TWO DESPERATE GOURMET DINNERS (yours, mine or ours) and try to keep the majority of ingredients in your pantry at all times. You can then invite anyone, anytime, without even thinking about what to serve.

AS SOON AS THE DOORBELL RINGS, FORGET ABOUT DETAILS AND ENJOY YOUR GUESTS. That's why you invited them in the first place, remember?

ABOVE ALL, HAVE A GOOD TIME MAKING OTHER PEOPLE HAPPY!

· INDEX ·